Sylvia J

W9-BMD-505

Building Your Organization's TQM System

Also available from ASQC Quality Press

Insights to Performance Excellence 1997: An Inside Look at the 1997 Baldrige Award Criteria
Mark L. Blazey

Quality Quotes
Hélio Gomes

Goldratt's Theory of Constraints: A Systems Approach to Continuous Improvement
H. William Dettmer

Mapping Work Processes
Dianne Galloway

Understanding and Applying Value-Added Assessment: Eliminating Business Process Waste
William E. Trischler

Avoiding the Pitfalls of Total Quality
Charles C. Poirier and Steven J. Tokarz

The Quality Toolbox
Nancy R. Tague

To request a complimentary catalog of publications, call 800-248-1946.

Building Your Organization's TQM System

The Unified Total Quality Model

Clarence Burns

ASQC Quality Press
Milwaukee, Wisconsin

Building Your Organization's TQM System: The Unified Quality Model
Clarence Burns

Library of Congress Cataloging-in-Publication Data
Burns, Clarence, 1944–
    Building your organization's TQM system: the unified total
quality model / Clarence Burns.
        p.   cm.
    Includes bibliographical references and index.
    ISBN 0-87389-422-7 (alk. paper)
    1. Total quality management.   I. Title.
HD62.15.B865   1997
658.5'62 — dc21   97-7863
                                                            CIP

Trademark Acknowledgment
Many of the designations used by manufacturers and sellers to distinguish their
products are claimed as trademarks. Where these designations appear in this
book and ASQC Quality Press was aware of a trademark claim, the designations
have been printed in initial caps.

10 9 8 7 6 5 4 3 2 1

ISBN 0-87389-422-7

Acquisitions Editor: Roger Holloway
Project Editor: Jeanne W. Bohn

ASQC Mission: To facilitate continuous improvement and increase customer
satisfaction by identifying, communicating, and promoting the use of quality
principles, concepts, and technologies; and thereby be recognized throughout
the world as the leading authority on, and champion for, quality.

Attention: Schools and Corporations
ASQC Quality Press books, videotapes, audiotapes, and software are available at
quantity discounts with bulk purchases for business, educational, or instructional
use. For information, please contact ASQC Quality Press at 800-248-1946, or
write to ASQC Quality Press, P.O. Box 3005, Milwaukee, WI 53201-3005.

For a free copy of the ASQC Quality Press Publications Catalog, including ASQC
membership information, call 800-248-1946.

Printed in the United States of America

∞ Printed on acid-free paper

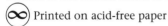

Quality Press
611 East Wisconsin Avenue
Milwaukee, Wisconsin 53202

Contents

Preface

This is not just a total quality management (TQM) how-to-do-it book. Nor does it just document TQM failures and how to correct them. It's not a book introducing the next important quality management movement. This book provides a unified theory for all this quality "stuff" going on around us. With the insight that a total quality practitioner—whether a trainer, team facilitator, executive, or consultant—can gain from the unified model, TQM implementation can be made easier and failures can be analyzed and corrected. Stephen W. Hawking (1988, 11) in *A Brief History of Time* states that "The eventual goal of science is to provide a single theory that describes the whole universe." What I present herein is a single unifying theory that describes the quality universe.

The unified theory will be introduced as the TQM triad, the unified total quality model (see Figure P.1). This model unifies and constructs a logically ordered whole from the multitudinous and sometimes seemingly conflicting methodologies, theories, and philosophies of the quality movement. There are many pieces to this jigsaw puzzle, and the three-circle model is a picture of the assembled TQM puzzle.

Many observers of the quality movement see an alphabet soup of programs, with shifting definitions and practices from expert to expert. There seems to be very little agreement on any-

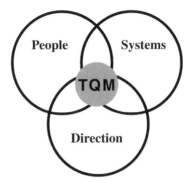

Figure P.1: *The TQM triad—The unified total quality model.*
Source: *Burns 1994.*

thing, from definitions for quality and TQM to what is needed for the creation of world-class quality organizations. With this tangled system, how can we effectively benchmark, network, or even communicate? The TQM triad provides the overall picture of the balance between various constituent quality programs needed to produce a total quality environment. The act of planning and managing the activities, strategies, and training to create that operating environment is an important component of total quality management.

If a model like the TQM triad is not employed when attempting to understand the plethora of quality programs out there, one can quickly become confused. Which guru or expert is right? What should we do now to stay or become competitive? Why is the staff making fun of our program-of-the-year club? Why do I feel like I'm living in a Dilbert comic strip?

The unified total quality model connects all the methodologies and philosophies from all the quality experts in such a way as to build understanding, not confusion. Frequently, misunderstanding or confusion develops because the giver and receiver of information are figuratively standing in different circles of the model. Understanding the interconnection of the quality programs will create a TQM strategy of building one step at a time instead of throwing out the past structure and restarting each time something new comes along. Continually changing programs causes negative reactions that can be far-reaching, deep, and long-lived. Combining, blending, and building on each successive program produces added dividends of synergy.

This book applies to all organizations: manufacturing, service, health care, education, and government. This unified total quality model can serve as a catalyst to initiate, restart, or improve an organization's TQM efforts. The intended audience spans the full spectrum of total quality practitioners, whether the reader's title is executive, manager, trainer, team leader, team member, or consultant. Each member of the organization can derive benefits from the knowledge gained by employing the model.

How can the unifying effect of the TQM triad benefit you? If you are a trainer, facilitator, or internal consultant, the introduction of new material can now be logically tied to what has gone before. Your ongoing efforts become focused, not just one disconnected new program after another, but a well thought out flow of continuing education. Questions about the seemingly conflicting statements by various quality experts can be answered in a positive sense, without having to argue that one is right and one is wrong. Which quality definition is the correct one? The model actually demonstrates that multiple definitions are acceptable; in fact, they are necessary. Thousands of dollars can be saved by not duplicating portions of past training, but building on them. I know an organization that trained its staff in three separate but similar problem-solving processes over a five-year period because a "new" problem-solving process was included with each new quality program it implemented.

Executives and managers can develop and explain cohesive quality management strategies. If you stated last year that continuous quality improvement was the process your organization was going to embrace, why are you now introducing reengineering? If quality circles were so great, why are you now pushing continuous quality improvement teams? Why do we need to implement this new buzzword program? The unified total quality model will make sense out of all this.

If you are an independent consultant or trainer, you can position your material and services within the context of the TQM triad. This allows you to provide a positive presentation of what you can add to an organization's TQM implementation. Also, your prospective clients will understand how your services will blend with their current quality improvement processes. This is much more believable than using a negative approach or promising a panacea.

Chapter 1 introduces the unified total quality model. TQM is defined as the unification of all quality management methodologies that can be positioned in one or more of the three circles of the model. Each component of TQM, represented by a circle, produces an important measurable result of an effective TQM process.

Chapter 2 demonstrates the unifying capabilities of the TQM triad. The three-part model accepts seemingly diverse and inconsistent quality definitions by placing each in its proper circle. There are also methodologies and philosophies that appear to be in conflict that can be brought into harmony with the model. A viable TQM system is dynamic—it must have the ability to grow, evolve, and continuously improve itself.

Chapter 3 illustrates how many of the inconsistencies perceived in quality programs and between quality experts dissolve when viewed within the context of the TQM triad. Management residing in the direction circle holds responsibility for ensuring the right things are done by the organization. The processes for doing those right things right reside in the systems and people circles. The model can also eliminate the tendency to get caught up in the program-of-the-year panacea search, an effort soon followed by the creation of the fad of last year.

Chapters 4 through 7 discuss each component circle of the model and the interactions between the circles. Each component has a unique measure of success, a unique quality definition, and specific total quality methodologies. Certain methodologies are defined as communicators between the component circles. Balancing quality improvement activities in each of the three triad components is discussed. This balance between the people and systems circles can be different, depending on the type of business being managed.

Chapter 8 presents some ideas for making the unified total quality model work for you and your organization. Hoshin planning is introduced as a powerful methodology of the TQM system. Its ability to drive breakthrough improvements is discussed within the context of the TQM triad. ISO 9000 series quality standards are positioned as guides for developing a quality assurance system at the operational level of the extended TQM triad. The Malcolm Baldrige National Quality Award is discussed as a diagnostic tool for the assessment of an organization's unified approach to TQM implementation. The TQM triad can also be used to effectively communicate with consultants, trainers, and the organization's workers.

Triad theorems are interspersed throughout the text. Each is a key point relating to the discussion preceding that theorem. Many of them are written within the context of the three circles of the TQM triad and represent statements of good quality management practice. A collection of all 20 theorems is in the appendix.

For future brevity in this book, I will use the word *program* to indicate a system encompassing the methodologies, philosophies, activities, theories, and tools of the subject under discussion — for example, a CQI program or a reengineering program. This usage is in the context of describing or labeling the system being implemented, not the description of the actual operation of the system or program, which would be a process. In other words, once installed in an organization, programs operate as ongoing processes.

Also for future brevity, I will drop the word *circle* whenever it seems appropriate in the discussion of the three-circle model and when it does not affect the clarity of the sentence. The three circles of the TQM triad will be referred to as Direction, People, and Systems — capitalized to indicate reference to the model.

Finally, I will be discussing concepts that may be new to some readers—for example, benchmarking, reengineering, cost of quality, or continuous quality improvement. I will briefly define these TQM methodologies as they are introduced in the material. Resources for further reading about these concepts can be found in the references. Also, I do not mean to imply that these are the only ingredients of an effective TQM system. The methodologies I have chosen are being used to demonstrate the functioning of the unified total quality model.

Good luck on your quality journey.

Acknowledgments

First, I am grateful to two people who were unknowing participants in the production of this book. Many times the really important learning doesn't take place in the classroom, but in the real world. John Balong was the quality professional that started me down this career path and gave me my first real-world training in quality improvement. This was an unusual case of having a mentor that reported to me in the organization — it was a rewarding experience.

When one ventures off into a training and consulting business, there must be that first important client. Neill Heitmann had the faith in me to offer the organization he worked for as that important first. I appreciate his continued assistance and friendship.

Next, thank you to the willing participants in this book production process, the editors and staff at ASQC Quality Press and the all-important volunteer members of the standing review board. The editors and staff at ASQC Quality Press were a joy to work with. They always had time to take my calls and answer my questions. ASQC Quality Press' manuscript review and book production processes are quality in practice. The reviewers who took their valuable time to read the manuscript and provided guidance for additions, changes, and corrections were greatly appreciated. The review process was an exercise in continuous improvement, and if it didn't end with zero defects I take total blame for the outcome.

And last of all, I wish to acknowledge the supporting participant, my wife Kate.

 **Chapter 1**

The Three Circles of the Unified Total Quality Model

Introduction

There are many pieces to the total quality management (TQM) jigsaw puzzle, with the three-circle model being a picture of the assembled puzzle. The circles represent the three components — people, systems, and direction — that must be present to provide a total quality management environment (see Figure 1.1). A unique balance of activities (depending on the type of organization being managed) in all three circles is needed to maximize the value from activities in any one of the circles. Customer satisfaction, continuous improvement, and growth potential are the outcomes generated by these three components. The overlap of the three circles symbolizes that the TQM triad forms a unique and unified business management approach where the effectiveness of each separate component is synergistically enhanced.

An Initial Overview of the TQM Triad

This has been an evolving model. When it was first introduced, only the people and systems circles were included. The important balance between the instruction offered by two trainers was being debated, one dealing with the people issues of team building and the other with the statistical problem-solving tools. The

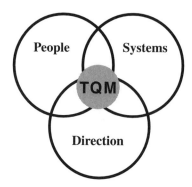

Figure 1.1: *The TQM triad—The unified total quality model.*
Source: *Burns 1994.*

model illustrated the uniqueness of each training package, but also how they connected and blended together. Later the third circle, Direction, was added to incorporate the role of management teachings such as those of Tom Peters and methodologies such as reengineering. When the model was used to introduce quality concepts in training sessions and to explain the interrelationship of quality programs, it seemed to decrease the confusion always present in new quality initiatives. (See the preface for an explanation of the use of the word *program* in this book.)

Quality methodologies, activities, and tools can be logically assigned to one of the three circles. Customer satisfaction surveys, team building, recognition, and employee empowerment are part of the people component. Problem solving, process analysis, prevention planning, and process measurement are included in the systems component. Developing mission and vision statements, planning business strategies, and reengineering are important activities in the direction component.

Most books, conferences, training sessions, and consultants are positioned in one of the three circles. I won't catalog all the possible quality program contributors and assign them to a circle, but give the reader the knowledge and understanding to do that. A program that does not contain material or include activities for each of the three components of the TQM triad is not deficient. Effective quality programs usually focus on just one component of the triad. This unified total quality model allows you to recognize which component is being covered by a quality program and plan for any additional balancing efforts that may be needed from the other two components.

Benefits of Using the TQM Triad

What are the benefits of being able to categorize the various quality programs that your organization has implemented or is planning to implement?

1. Eliminate confusion with the alphabet soup of quality programs.
2. Improve communication among total quality practitioners.
3. Provide balance between various TQM constituent programs.
4. Improve the acceptance of new training.
5. Eliminate redundant training.
6. Provide a foundation for a cohesive TQM strategy.
7. Facilitate selection of an independent consultant when a certain circle focus is needed.

How the unified total quality model can create these benefits will be discussed in the following chapters.

Models for Different Purposes

How do other TQM models compare with the unified total quality model? Existing models, and there are many, are either modeling a certain author's total quality definition, a TQM methodology, or a procedure to effectively implement TQM. These models cannot, however, be considered unifying models because they make no effort to show relationships with all the other total quality models, methodologies, philosophies, theories, and tools that are available to organizations striving to build an effective TQM system. On the whole, these models are valuable contributions to the quality movement, and this unified total quality model is not an attempt to supplant them, but to integrate them into a TQM system as important pieces of the puzzle.

One of the well-known models is the Juran Trilogy®, consisting of three interrelated processes: quality planning, quality control, and quality improvement (Juran 1989). This model is an excellent example of one that defines a quality management methodology focused on quality improvement. It utilizes activities and tools from all three circles of the TQM triad to accomplish that result.

J.M. Juran's model can be described within the context of the three circles. The *quality planning* process establishes production processes in the systems circle to produce goods and services that meet the identified customers' needs. These needs are determined through interaction with customers in the people circle. His *quality control* process measures and maintains process performance in the systems circle at acceptable levels based on quality goals. The *quality improvement* process is Juran's continuous improvement methodology that would reside in the systems circle and be driven by input from the direction circle.

Why isn't Juran's model a unifying model? The easy, but probably insufficient, answer is: That's not the objective of his model. The more complete answer is found by examining what is yet to come in this book. A unifying model accepts all methodologies, theories, and philosophies of the total quality movement and explains their interrelationship. The TQM triad will demonstrate this in discussions about reengineering, theory of constraints, cost of quality, benchmarking, continuous quality improvement, zero defects, and open-book management. The TQM triad will provide the total overall picture of the TQM system, while Juran's model provides necessary guidance for quality practitioners in how to effectively use certain elements of the TQM system.

A recently published book by Joseph Kelada (1996) introduces a model he calls the *total quality triad,* similar in name but very different in concept from the unified total quality model, the TQM triad. His model depicts the interaction of a company's people, customers, and shareholders. Three qualities are superimposed on his triad corresponding with the three groups: quality of life for people, a quality experience for customers,

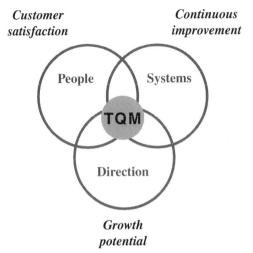

Figure 1.2: *The TQM triad results or outcomes.*
Source: *Burns 1994.*

and quality returns for the shareholders. These three groups of people and their corresponding quality objectives are related to the outcomes of the TQM triad (see Figure 1.2). All three circles will affect the quality of life of the organization's people, especially with the emphasis on the internal customer interactions in the people circle. The people circle will also have the major role in providing a quality experience for the customer. It can be demonstrated that all three circles' outcomes will positively affect the quality of shareholders' returns.

Who Makes TQM Work?

The discussion so far has been about programs and models—that is, where the various methodologies, processes, tools, and philosophies of the total quality movement fit in the TQM triad. What about the people in the systems and processes created by these quality programs? All workers in an organization have positions in the triad, depending on the process that they are operating at any given time.

The People Circle. *Individuals* are working in the people circle when they are involved in process activities that require interaction with internal or external customers. Everyone in the organization spends a portion of each working day in these activities since all work involves a process and all processes have internal and/or external customers. The attributes and activities of the people circle will be more fully developed in chapter 6.

The Systems Circle. *Teams* are usually found in the systems circle, working on problem-solving and process improvement projects. The systems and their associated processes that are represented in this component of the triad have been designed initially and are continuously improved with information about customer requirements gained through interactions in the people circle. The attributes and activities in the systems circle will be discussed in chapter 5.

The Direction Circle. This circle is *management* territory, where decisions are made on innovative products, services, and business processes. Actions taken here provide jobs for the people circle and require systems to be designed for the systems circle. This circle will be discussed further in chapter 4.

Results from Each Component of the TQM Triad

In this section we will take an introductory look at the result generated by each component of the TQM triad by using an example process that resides in that component. Note the shift from program to process. Once a program is installed and operating, it becomes a process.

People Circle

The cycle of plan-do-check-act (PDCA) can be used to explain the basic activities in this component of the triad. *Plan* the processes to produce outcomes that satisfy customers. What are the needs, expectations, and requirements of the customers? *Do* the process and deliver the output to the customers. *Check* the results by measuring customer satisfaction. *Act* on the feedback from the customer.

Developing people's skills in the listening and communication process would occur in this circle. The result would be an expected increase in customer satisfaction. This increase could be from an organization's employees interacting in a more pleasing manner with external customers or from improving internal customer–supplier relationships. Customer satisfaction as the outcome of the people component is consistent with the placement of individuals in this circle as opposed to teams. One-on-one interactions with internal and external customers are the settings for improving customer satisfaction.

Systems Circle

Probably the most popular of the TQM processes is the continuous quality improvement (CQI) process.

> *Continuous quality improvement:* An organization-wide, team-based approach to developing and improving systems, processes, products, and services, based on a thorough understanding of customers' needs and expectations; using the methodologies of process analysis, statistical measurement, and problem solving.

In the systems circle the PDCA cycle is customarily enhanced with a more rigorous approach of a stepwise problem-solving technique. An operating system generating nonconformances or otherwise operating inefficiently is attacked by a CQI team wielding the problem-solving tools to produce measurable improvement. The continual repetition of this activity generates the result of continuous improvement.

Note that the outcome from this circle is continuous improvement, not incremental improvement. This model does not differentiate methodologies and place them in different circles based on the percentage of improvement, either expected or accrued. I do place CQI and reengineering in different circles, but not because of falsely perceived differences in possible implementation payoffs. The definition for improvement used in this model is best stated by Juran (1989, 28), *"Improvement* means the organized creation of beneficial change; the attainment of unprecedented levels of performance. A synonym is *breakthrough.*"

Direction Circle

The process of developing business strategies that produce, first, the potential for organizational growth, and second, the results of customer satisfaction and continuous improvement, resides in this circle. These business strategies would relate to what markets to enter, what products and services to offer, and how to present the offerings to the customer. Activities in this component have a high risk attached but, if successful, can provide excellent organizational growth. Deciding to develop a brand-new technology commercially, to offer a new or existing service with an innovative approach, or to reengineer a major business process can have enormous payback—or be the first step to oblivion. Remember People Express airline, Beta VCRs, and the DeLorean automobile? Some readers might question the inclusion of these activities in a TQM model, but the output of this process has profound effects on the other two circles, as indicated by the secondary results just mentioned. Also, some of the important authors and other quality leaders in the TQM movement specifically address issues that are part of this process.

Interconnected Results

One important guideline for deciding the placement of a quality program in the TQM triad will be the expected result of the implementation of that program. Secondary results usually exist and are represented by the overlap of the circles. One can say that continuous improvement produces customer satisfaction and growth, or that improving customer satisfaction is a form of continuous improvement. It can also be said that growth potential makes the other two results possible. So not only are there secondary results, but all the results are tightly linked together.

> ### *Triad Theorem 1: TQM is not three divergent methodologies forced together in a three-segment pie diagram, but three interlocking circles that interact with each other synergistically.*

A Road Map or a Guidebook

During the writing of this book its draft subtitle was *A Guidebook for Your Quality Journey*. The word *guidebook* was chosen instead of *road map* for a specific reason. *Road map* used in the context of many quality books seems to mean: Here is the route to success in continuous quality improvement, reengineering, or whatever quality subject a particular author might be writing about. The problem with this type of road map is the assumption that there is just one right way to get from point A to point B. If you believe as Eileen Shapiro (1995, 181), author of *Fad Surfing in the Boardroom*, does, "that no one knows a priori the exact way for your organization to make these changes [changes created by the adoption of a TQM approach], then you cannot reasonably expect a cookbook answer to be satisfactory." A true road map shows many roads that can be taken to reach a destination. The successes in TQM implementation that have been reported seem to indicate that each organization has probably taken its own unique route to reach a common destination, although one could also argue that each has arrived at its own unique destination.

> ### *Triad Theorem 2: Every organization will take its own unique route to its own unique TQM system—throw away your cookbooks.*

Leaders of organizations are probably best suited to choose the route and the destination that will be their organization's unique TQM experience. What I hope to do is to provide a guidebook to assist you in planning your journey. Knowing how quality programs fit into the unified total quality model and interconnect with each other will allow you to customize your TQM system. Gaining the ability to blend future quality programs that you may undertake, with your present TQM system, will make the overall effort less intimidating. In addition, the ability to coherently explain your total quality journey to your staff gives the seemingly separate programs some continuity and puts a strong understandable structure into your overall management system.

As the TQM practitioner gains understanding of the triad, he or she will be able to place new or emerging tools or methodologies in the correct circle. Knowing the attributes of each circle will make this easier—this guidebook will provide that knowledge with a tour through the three-circle model. The TQM triad can also highlight the need for a certain quality program that may be missing from your present TQM system—for instance, the need to have cost of quality as a communication tool between the systems and direction circles.

TQM Defined by the Unified Total Quality Model

This unified model does not constrain you from developing personalized definitions for your organization. Here is an example definition for TQM based on the model.

> *Total quality management:* A business management approach with an unfaltering focus on the outcomes of customer satisfaction, continuous improvement, and growth potential. These outcomes are generated by improving the quality of an organization's customer service, products, services, and profits.

Many existing TQM definitions originate from the background and perspective of where the author of the definition is standing in the model. That is, if one is specifically focused on process improvement, one's definition will reflect this position. Another person who strongly believes in customer satisfaction, possibly at the exclusion of continuous improvement methodologies, will embrace a definition that highlights the relationship of customer satisfaction with TQM. A survey of definitions found in the numerous quality books and journals illustrates this basic problem in the TQM movement: We can't even agree on what it is! Without consistency in a descriptive definition, any concept—valid as it may be—becomes lost in confusion. With very little agreement on a definition, how can we effectively communicate among quality professionals, let alone try to explain TQM to someone new to the subject? One organization used this questionable approach to eliminate the problem: "We believe that the term total quality management (TQM), along with similar concepts and phrases, actually hindered the progress of our improvement efforts, so today we have no definition for TQM. We try to avoid any type of quality jargon in referring to the way we operate" (Landes 1995, 44). This may have been overkill to overcome the inconsistency in what the quality jargon means to different practitioners. We don't have to use exactly the same words, we just need to be explaining the same system.

Is TQM Another Name for CQI?

Some definitions focus only on the systems-circle activities, having continuous improvement as the only or principal ingredient. Here are some examples of this type of definition found in the literature.

> TQM is a strategic architecture requiring evaluation and refinement of continuous improvement practices in all areas of a business. (Roosevelt 1995, 35)

> TQM is the continuous improvement of all activities. It is a methodology as well as a way of life. It encompasses such tools and techniques as statistical process control, goal alignment, and failure mode effects analysis, while channeling the mind-set of every employee to achieve continuous improvement. (Rau 1995, 57)

These definitions are loose enough that someone could argue that continuous improvement also encompasses a focus on customer satisfaction and growth. Investigation of the activities in organizations following these definitions usually leads one to the conclusion that the effort is the traditional CQI approach: teams solving problems with the application of statistical tools and a formal problem-solving routine.

Limiting the definition to only incorporate continuous quality improvement puts an unnecessary constraint on the quality programs available to an organization as part of a cohesive TQM package. If a program does not directly result in continuous quality improvement, does that mean it's not TQM oriented? A business espousing a continuous improvement style of a TQM definition would be perceived by its workers as shifting focus from TQM if upper management decided to initiate a customer service quality program. Reengineering is not about continuous improvement; hence, if CQI and TQM are defined as the same system, reengineering would be excluded. A false dichotomy has been set up. Then the oft-heard battle starts — Which is better? Which way should the organization proceed? TQM or reengineering? One methodology may win, but the organization loses. Expanding the TQM definition to cover all three circles of the TQM triad will bring both CQI and reengineering under the total quality umbrella, and the problem of what is and is not TQM is eliminated.

Is TQM a Customer Satisfaction Program?

Writers of other definitions remember that to remain in business we must satisfy the customer. Now the people component is added to the definition.

> TQM is a management philosophy that builds a customer-driven, learning organization dedicated to total customer satisfaction through continuous improvement in the effectiveness and efficiency of the organization and its processes. (Corrigan 1995, 61)

TQM is responsive customer service through continuously improved and redesigned work processes. (Buch and Shelnutt 1995, 73)

Again, I want to emphasize the importance of having a definition for TQM that fits your organization's needs but addresses all three components of the model. If your definition has a focus on only one or two components of the model, problems can develop. Use your own words to capture the umbrella aspect of TQM.

Triad Theorem 3: You pick the color, but make sure your TQM definition is an umbrella.

In this chapter, I've attempted to give you insight into the unified total quality model to enable you to understand the applications and examples that follow. As the model is further developed, its application to your processes will become clearer, and the TQM puzzle will start to come together.

 **Chapter 2**

Diversity Unified

Introduction

In chapter 1 the unified total quality model was used to clarify the differences in the definitions for TQM and CQI. Now it will be used to provide some consistency and order for definitions of quality. As with the situation for TQM definitions, there are also many definitions for quality. The difference is that where many of the TQM definitions were too restrictive, most of the quality definitions are acceptable within the context of the three-circle model. All the seemingly diverse definitions for quality can be logically integrated by placing each in its proper circle of the triad. The definition for quality really hasn't changed over time, just the focus on a specific circle, which in turn carries with it a unique collection of definitions.

In addition to bringing all the quality definitions under one umbrella, the TQM triad joins together apparently conflicting quality-related methodologies. In fact, the only real conflict may be that caused by the inference that a certain methodology is the singular requirement for a viable TQM system. When a model is available that allows room for and links the different methodologies, the conflicts disappear and are replaced with a broader understanding of a holistic TQM approach.

The chapter closes with a look to the future. New quality programs will surely be introduced if past trends continue. The TQM triad integrates these developing quality technologies into an organization's evolving TQM system, giving the system the ability to continuously improve itself as well as the organization.

More Than One Definition of Quality Is Okay

To take full advantage of the TQM triad's ability to place the quality definitions and, in general, all quality programs within a meaningful context, more structure must first be added to the model.

The Operational Level

The TQM system and associated processes can only be implemented within an existing operating organization: management (Direction), providing strategies and resources; teams (Systems), operating systems and processes; and individuals (People), interacting with internal and external customers. This operational level is represented by a second set of circles (see Figure 2.1). These six circles become the extended TQM triad model.

The operational-level primary outputs from the three sets of processes are (1) management strategies causing profits, (2) systems producing products and services, and (3) people providing customer service. This may seem to be an oversimplification of how an organization operates, but as one adds levels of complexity to running a business, the model still works. The effort here is to tie everything together, so I'll keep it simple to make the correlations with the model easier to observe.

Most likely, even at the operational level without TQM, some of the TQM outcomes are generated: customer satisfaction, continuous improvement, and growth potential. Without a structured TQM approach, however, the results are inconsistent and usually focused on growth at all costs. When no TQM system is present, self-defeating activities occur such as adding inspection step after inspection step to eliminate defects, huge workforce cutbacks to increase short-term profits, and satisfying the

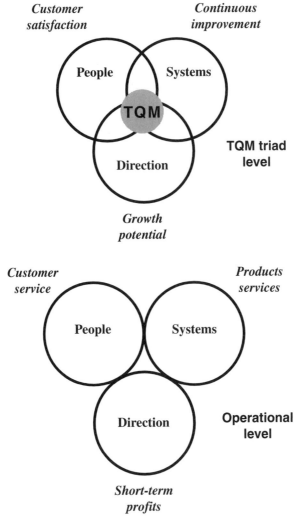

Figure 2.1: The two levels of the extended triad model.

dissatisfied customer with major giveaways with no thought toward eliminating the root causes of the problem.

The three circles used as a model for the operations of an organization without TQM could be thought of as just touching and not overlapping. TQM is the force that brings the three seemingly separate areas together into an efficient, growing, and profitable operation. With the three circles intermeshed, the outputs (profit, products, and customer service) become better because they are strongly affected by the outcomes (growth potential, continuous improvement, and customer satisfaction) of the TQM business management approach. In future discussions in this book, both the components of the operational level and the TQM triad level will be addressed.

Measurable Quality Operationally Defined

Quality is a measure of a special characteristic of the output of the processes residing in each circle at the operational level. Generically we could label this special characteristic as a degree of excellence, fitness for use, or product integrity. These generic descriptions can be worrisome for the quality professional who seeks a measurable quality definition. Quality as "I'll know it when I see it" just isn't good enough. Therefore, as quality definitions are enumerated for each circle, an attempt will be made to provide definitions that can be operationally defined. W. Edwards Deming (1993, 108) describes an operational definition as "a procedure agreed upon for translation of a concept into measurement of some kind." An operational definition will provide a systematic procedure for acquiring meaningful data and eliminate the subjectivity inherent in many measurements. The following points are the basic requirements of an operational definition (Ball 1992).

1. Define the characteristic to be measured.
2. Choose a measurement device.
3. Describe the method for measurement.
4. State the decision criteria for evaluation of the resulting measurements.

Examples of operational definitions for quality will be given in the following chapters that examine each circle in detail.

Quality in the Systems Circle

An organization's products and services come into being as the output of the systems residing in this circle at the operational level. The customer, whether the final customer or the next person or department in your organization, has certain needs and

expectations of the product or service, which must be transformed as accurately and completely as possible into customer
requirements. Some of the expectations may be hard to capture
as requirements and may have to be addressed by customer
satisfaction activities in the people circle. Customer interviews
using a tool that provides for a structured and documented requirements check may surface previously unknown requirements. Customer satisfaction surveys, on the other hand, may
indicate problem areas but they will not find missing requirements. The systems, in turn, must be designed and operated to
produce output that meets these requirements. The quality definition for the systems circle becomes *meeting the customers' requirements*. This is a customer-driven approach to quality that
can be measured and managed.

Certainly, other definitions exist that belong in this circle.
Some focus on zero defects as a goal — for instance, *quality as
"freedom from deficiencies."* (This is one of the two definitions
addressed by Juran, the other being "product features that meet
customer needs" [Juran 1989, 16].) The definition, in whatever
form, must be customer driven and based on measurable requirements. If your definition fits these criteria, it probably is
a systems-circle definition. In this definition, requirements, defects, or deficiencies are not just referring to product or service
attributes (specifications), but also consistency, pricing, scheduling, handling, packaging, and servicing after the sale, to name
a few. What this means is that requirements are derived from
two major sources, the product or service specifications and the
customers' expectations. An example of a customer expectation
is: I expect the new automobile I just purchased to be delivered
in two days, properly serviced, washed, with a full tank of gas,
and, furthermore, if there are any problems, I expect immedi-
ate attention in the service department. I expect to be offered a
loaner car if mine must remain in the service department.

The Basic Level of Quality. This quality definition provides
a way to determine if the process output is quality or not, unit
by unit. The process operator and the customer possess consis-

tent measures of quality based on documented requirements, and the output performance can be measured, recorded, and charted by either party. It is absolutely necessary that everyone involved, whether supplier, process operator, or customer, understand what a quality product or service looks like. This is the *gatekeeper* definition for quality. Any unit of product or service that does not meet the customers' requirements should not be allowed to get to the customer, whether internal or external. No amount of customer service quality added to the product or service in the people circle makes up for requirements not being met. This definition provides a relatively static level of quality, but it can be revised as customer requirements change.

The quality definition for this circle of the TQM triad was introduced first for a purpose. It's the basic level of required quality. If your organization can't produce a product or service that meets customers' requirements, you may as well forget about ever improving customer satisfaction. An increased level of customer satisfaction, whether you label it customer delight or exceeding customer expectations, must be built on products and services that conform to the documented requirements. Tom Peters (1994, 229) says it this way, "These days, getting the quality right by the numbers, according to the statistical measures, amounts to no more than a pass for the player's entrance at the stadium; it doesn't put points on the board." If this basic level of quality only allows you to gain access to the game, many organizations are still outside the stadium looking in. An organization must master the methodologies, tools, and techniques of the systems circle, specifically the CQI process, to get the quality right by the numbers.

Quality—An Operational-Level Attribute. Note that these example quality definitions are used at the operational level of the systems circle to monitor and measure the quality of process inputs and outputs. If nonconformities, excess variation, or other problems are noted in the product flow, the CQI methodologies of the systems circle at the TQM level are employed to improve the product and service quality at the operational level

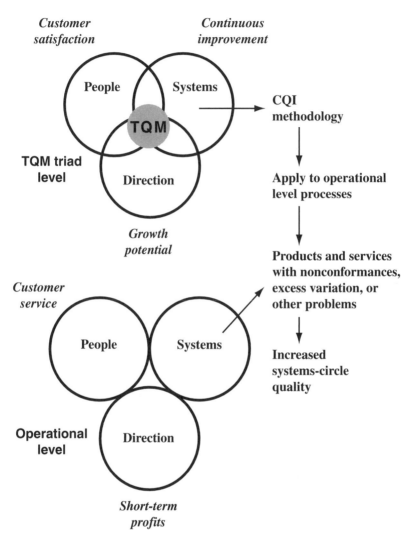

Figure 2.2: *CQI from the TQM triad level interacting with processes at the operational level to produce increased product and service quality.*

(see Figure 2.2). That is, if we start by saying quality is meeting the customers' requirements, the first step is establishing and documenting these requirements. Then second, process measurements signal that we have not met the customers' requirements. Implementing a CQI project team with a zero defects performance standard will move us toward quality defined as meeting customers' requirements. This interaction between the quality definition of the operational level and the concept of CQI at the TQM triad level addresses an inconsistency that has concerned some quality professionals.

Some in quality management have always felt there was a conflict between the *requirements* definition for quality and the concept of continuous quality improvement. Using a comparison of quality and profit explains the difference between and shows the compatibility of the definition and CQI. Just as we need to define profit to assist in pricing goods and services, we need to define quality to accept and ship goods or set guidelines for services. After acceptable profit is defined and the process is set in place to cause it, there is ongoing pressure to improve it. The same is true with quality. What we deliver today can be defined as a quality product or service, but we know only continuous improvement of the process will keep us in the game with the competition.

Quality as meeting customer requirements is the measure of the output of the process, while CQI is the means to improve the process. An organization must embrace both concepts to improve products and services for the customer.

Quality in the People Circle

Quality definitions for this circle are harder to nail down. They usually are not measurable against something like customer requirements. In the people circle, discussing high and low quality seems to have some meaning, while in the systems circle there is no degree of quality. A product or service either meets customer requirements or it does not. High and low as relative quality levels make no sense when discussing systems output of products or services.

The following two definitions for service quality would fit in the people circle of the triad: *quality of service*—exceeding customers' expectations for service, and, from the book by Valarie Zeithaml, A. Parasuraman, and Leonard Berry, *Delivering Quality Service* (1990, 19), "the extent of discrepancy between customers' expectations or desires and their perceptions." Where the systems-circle quality definition was the gatekeeper, this definition is the *differentiator*. An organization operating without this added quality has just a commodity for a product or service and is doomed to price-war competition.

Once again, as in the systems circle, these definitions are used at the operational level to monitor and measure the quality of the process output, customer service. If customer service is unacceptable, the customer satisfaction methodologies of the people circle at the TQM level are employed to increase customer service quality at the operational level.

With service quality so defined, and I don't offer a better way, it is possible for only the customer to measure it—not the supplier. The supplier of the service can come along after the delivery of the service and only then ask the customer for feedback. Remember that with product and service quality from the systems circle, both the customer and supplier could measure it.

Two Types of Service. To prevent confusion, let's differentiate between *service* as used in the systems circle and *customer service* as used in the people circle. Systems-circle service is defined as one of the possible outputs of an organization's processes. This service is what is being sold, and it has been defined in the previous section. In this category of service both the customer and supplier can measure quality. Examples would be getting a carpet cleaned, a lawn mowed, or a haircut; taking an airplane trip; securing a loan; or buying stock.

Customer service as used in the people circle refers to the presentation, delivery, and follow-up after the sale of a product or service. As the supplier, we can be creative and innovative in this area, but we can't measure the results until the customer has experienced the customer service and formed a perception of how we did. High customer service quality then is the experience of having perceived the customer service provided as much better than was expected, hence, customer delight. Of course, the next time this same customer experiences the same customer service, his or her expectations will have been raised by the past positive experience. For example, once I had arrived late at a hotel, so I decided to order a meal from room service. The person answering the phone already knew my name and used it. Wow! Certainly the technology exists to perform this magic trick, but I had just checked in—the process was fast. This simple little action would become one of the sum of many that formed my perception and caused it to be higher than my expectations going into the experience. Of course, using my name became part of my expectations, and the next day when room service didn't use my name I felt slighted.

Tracing the flow of activities from continuous improvement to a delighted customer illustrates how the TQM triad models the creation of world-class customer satisfaction. First, in the systems circle, continuous improvement shifts the system toward the production of output that meets all the customers' requirements. The overlapping area shared by the systems and people circles represents the effect of continuous improvement on customer satisfaction. Reaching the level of just meeting the customers' requirements establishes the baseline of customer satisfaction. Then empowered employees, through implementation of customer satisfaction methodologies residing in the people circle, generate a higher level of perceived quality. This in turn creates the opportunity to delight customers.

Quality in the Direction Circle

Quality definitions for this circle are not often discussed. If we are to use quality to measure the output of the direction circle at the operational level, as we did with the other two circles, then in this circle we are looking at profit quality. How do we measure profit quality? It's not the quantity of profit any more than the quality of the product in the systems circle is represented by the quantity of parts produced.

Profit quality is affected by actions in all three circles and, in that, differs from the concepts of quality in the people and systems circles. Improved product and service quality in the systems circle can positively affect profitability. Improved customer service quality in the people circle can affect profitability. Finally, actions taken in the direction circle, such as selecting new markets to enter and planning the introduction of innovative products and services, directly affect the organization's profitability.

Profit quality also requires a strong linkage between the circles. Decisions in the direction circle relating to quality profit generation can't be made without regard to the possible consequences in or synergy with the other two circles. There is an interrelationship here that cannot be neglected by an organization striving for quality profits. Profits not based on long-term action in all three circles are not quality profits, as is being proved by the shortsighted efforts to improve profits by downsizing.

Many organizations have no concept of a quality definition for profit. This could be a serious flaw with TQM practiced without a unified three-circle model. While workers and teams are diligently practicing TQM methodologies in the people and systems circles, management in the direction circle can be making decisions and taking actions completely contrary to good TQM practices concerning quality profits. The following are examples of profit generating activities that many times create nonquality profit.

1. Downsizing—cutting a significant percentage of workers without changing the business processes
2. Eliminating all training not directly related to production of the product or service
3. Getting wage concessions from workers

Actions such as these that have no regard for the other two circles cause negative ramifications in an organization's TQM efforts.

***Triad Theorem 4: Actions in one circle
that negatively impact the other two circles
are counterproductive to TQM and
produce nonquality outcomes.***

Tying Together Other Diverse Methodologies

The model has just demonstrated its usefulness by tying together seemingly inconsistent or conflicting quality definitions. There also exists many diverse methodologies, some of them supposedly in conflict, that can be brought into accord with the TQM triad. The area of service quality improvement previously discussed will be restudied in more detail. The methodologies used to improve customer service and the resultant customer satisfaction can be derailed by some of the misunderstandings that presently exist.

Service Revisited: Service as a Product and Customer Service

We've all heard that America has become a service-based economy. Statements like "90 percent of new jobs are in the service sector" describe the dynamics of the mix related to the systems circle. What that statement says is that at the operational level, more of the systems' outputs are becoming services, not products.

The definition of service quality in the systems circle is no different than the definition for product quality. Many quality practitioners tend to mix this service quality with that of customer service quality, which derives from the people circle. These are two entirely different concepts from two different circles of the triad, with two different ways of measuring results. Not every business is classified as a service business, but every business does deliver customer service both internally and externally.

A business differentiates itself from the competition in the systems circle with technological advantages and in the people circle with innovative customer service benefits. The dividing line between service quality and customer service quality is not fixed since, as was indicated previously, customer service benefits can turn into service requirements. As the innovations of the people circle become expected and standard throughout the industry, they no longer offer a competitive advantage, but move to the systems circle and become customer requirements. If a computer retailer decides to add in-home setup as a customer service benefit, it can gain a competitive advantage. The difference between the customers' perceptions and their expectations of the customer service becomes greater—in other words, customer satisfaction increases. When every retailer in the shopping area offers the same benefit of in-home setup, the benefit becomes a customer expectation that will be reflected as an added service requirement.

Service Business or Manufacturing Business: Is There a Difference? Differentiating organizations or even departments based on whether their output is a product or a service may be an interesting exercise for the economist concerned about the U.S. job market, but it has very little to do with quality in the systems circle. Whether you deliver a Boeing 777 airplane or a vacation flight to Tahiti, a Ford automobile or a taxi ride to the airport, defining and producing quality output in the systems circle is the same. Customers expect their requirements concerning specifications, cost, on-time delivery, and safety to be met.

The differentiation the quality professional is concerned with occurs in the people circle and is the result of customer service differences among competing businesses. Customer service is just as important whether your systems output is a product or a service. So in the final analysis, there really is no difference between a service business and a manufacturing business when it comes to TQM.

Using the previous insight based on the application of the unified total quality model, let's analyze some issues listed by Zeithaml, Parasuraman, and Berry (1990, 16). These authors have noted three emerging themes from the service quality literature. The first refers to quality as measured in the systems circle: "Service quality is more difficult for customers to evaluate than goods [what this book is calling products] quality." They state as an example of this theme that it is more complicated to evaluate a stockbroker's offered investment services than home insulation materials, relative to service quality. This is dealing with the previously discussed false dichotomy in the systems circle.

Isn't this just an excuse for not being able to identify and document customers' requirements, an activity long practiced by manufacturers?

The second emerging theme addresses customer service quality as measured in the people circle: "Customers do not evaluate service quality solely on the outcome of a service (e.g., how a customer's hair looks after a haircut); they also consider the process of service delivery" (1990, 16). Is this to imply that customers of products do not also evaluate the product based on the process of customer service during delivery? We know that's not true. Once again the literature seems to be attempting to construct a dichotomy, now in the people circle, where none exists. In both of these themes a differentiation is being assumed between products and services using the apparent dissimilarities of their quality and customer service quality definitions. An understanding derived from the triad clearly demonstrates that there is no difference.

The third emerging theme is the only one that doesn't deal with a false dichotomy. It relates to the definition of quality in the people circle, comparing perception to expectations to get the customers' judgment on service quality. The use of *service quality* to also include customer service quality, however, does tend to complicate comprehension, as it does also in the second theme.

It has been shown that the methodologies related to producing product and service quality and the methodologies related to producing customer service quality are linked in the TQM triad as the interconnecting people and systems circles. Whether the item being produced and delivered is a product or a service, the methodologies to cause quality are the same.

Reengineering and CQI: A Powerful Combination

(See chapter 4 for a definition of *reengineering*.) The contribution of the TQM triad to this combination of methodologies is to place them in separate circles, both under the TQM umbrella. If CQI and reengineering are considered as programs within TQM, the discussion can refocus on the positioning of them in the model so as to gain maximum advantage from both. Too many in upper management seem to be taking the following approach—we tried TQM (CQI), we were discouraged with the results, now we are doing reengineering. In fact, the two programs support each other when both are implemented and continued in the organization. Management controls the use of reengineering in the direction circle, while quality improvement leaders, facilitators, and teams manage and implement the CQI process in the systems circle. Both can be in place and functioning at the same time. The only thing to be cautious of would be to not reengineer and use CQI on the same process simultaneously.

After a business process has been reengineered, there is the potential for additional benefits to be gained by applying CQI. This might take the form of fine-tuning the process or process improvement to eliminate opportunities for error embedded in the new process. On the other hand, a process that had been improved by a CQI team may be a candidate for reengineering.

The TQM triad accepts diverse methodologies and coalesces them into a unified system. The emphasis is not on which methodology is better, but how to blend them and gain the synergy of the combinations. Chapter 3 will extend this discussion by exploring the interactions between zero defects and systems circle processes, reengineering and CQI, and cost of quality and the direction circle, all within the context of the unified total quality model.

Dynamics and Change in the TQM Triad

A TQM system must be dynamic and have the ability to change to remain a viable management system. Two aspects of this ability to respond to the changing needs of the organization are (1) the ability to add new quality programs as they are identified as opportunities for organizational growth, and (2) the ability to coalesce these new additions into an integrated whole. The first ability is that of facilitating change, and the second is that of providing the framework for dynamics between quality programs turned processes. The unified total quality model provides the guide to producing a TQM system with these two abilities.

A second area of dynamics in the TQM triad is the balance among the three circles. This triad balance has the following attributes: (1) it must be managed, (2) it changes over time, and (3) it is different for various types of organizations. Most of the balance that will be addressed is between the people and systems circles. Many organizations will heavily focus on methodologies in either the people or the systems circle, depending on the bent of the TQM leader and the type of organization. This imbalance must be recognized and managed by selecting a suitable balancing quality program in the other circle. For example, many TQM leaders and facilitators have a special affinity for the process analysis and problem-solving tools. They seem to believe that if they could just get all of their teams conversant with these tools, no problem would be unsolvable in their organization. Could it be that the reason their teams seem to be unproductive is that they need some people-skills training? Another example is the business, many times a retailer, that bends over backward in offering super customer service but hasn't the slightest idea of what continuous improvement can do for its processes. I'll revisit this topic in more detail in chapters 7 and 8.

A third dynamic in the TQM triad is the fact that TQM activities in one circle rely on and cause activities in the other two circles. A good example here would be the previous one. Generally, to positively affect customer service quality and thereby cause customer satisfaction in the people circle requires a reliance on the continuous improvement practices of the systems circle. Specifically, a problem discovered by a customer satisfaction survey should cause continuous quality improvement activities to eliminate the root causes.

The potential for dramatic change exists in all three circles, not just the direction circle. Empowering people can lead to quantum leaps in customer satisfaction, and implementing CQI teams can offer dramatic results in continuous improvement.

Triad Theorem 5: A viable TQM system has the ability to continuously improve itself.

 **Chapter 3**

Experts and Fads

Introduction

What's the connection between experts and fads? Experts are usually known for their own unique quality models, philosophies, and methodologies. In differentiating their TQM approaches from the competition, apparent disagreements are sometimes emphasized, or so it seems. To the CEO or manager looking for assistance in quality improvement, each of the experts' programs seems to be promoted as the pathway to a successful TQM system. The abundance of quality programs promoted in this fashion sets the stage for the development of the actions that create fads out of otherwise excellent programs. An organization's management, in its quest for an effective and successful TQM system, tends to jump from one program to another instead of continuously evolving its own unique system. The practice of selecting a new expert or program to follow every few years in the search for the panacea program creates the appearance of fads coming and going in the quality domain.

Disagreement Among the Experts

Proponents of CQI discount the value of reengineering. Reengineering advocates say theirs is a business revolution about radical improvement, and that TQM deals with incremental improvement (Hammer and Stanton 1995). Philip Crosby (1984) offers as his third absolute of four, the performance standard of zero defects (do it right the first time), while Deming (1986, 141) wrote of "the fallacy of zero defects." Peters (1995, 53) says, "Do it right the first time. Candidate for dumbest statement ever uttered by a human." Can all these seemingly conflicting statements by various experts all be right? Can the TQM triad unify these apparent differences?

Frequently these and many other misunderstandings develop because the context and, hence, the correct circle in the TQM triad are not identified. Also, many of the inconsistencies perceived in the quality movement can be eliminated when looked at within the context of the three-circle model.

Zero Defects—It's Not for Motivation

The quotes about zero defects (ZD) are a good example of the misunderstandings present in the total quality movement. Addressing ZD first should not be construed as an indication of its position of importance on the quality program menu. It is, however, an interesting example because of the strong positions taken for and against the concept by various quality leaders. In this case, the conflict is between the systems circle, where ZD resides, and the direction circle, where poor understanding and decisions by management can cause the failure of this approach. Deming had witnessed abuses of this philosophy and preferred to identify it as a fallacy. The abuses of ZD can be divided into two main problem categories, one emanating from the direction circle and one from the systems circle.

ZD Abused in the Direction Circle. Upper management has time and again treated ZD as a "motivation" program. Crosby (1984) emphatically states that ZD is not a motivation program—it's a quality management standard. It's a specific standard that tells people working in the organization's processes what is expected from them in their work. Used as a motivation program, it leads to asking people to pay more attention, work harder, and not make mistakes!—all exhortations that Deming (1986) wanted to see eliminated, as stated in his tenth of 14 management points. Empty words and management pressure to do it right the first time do not drive the necessary actions in the systems circle to produce continuous improvement. Instead, this turns out to be demotivating for the worker thrown into a process that is not capable of producing error-free output. The results from treating ZD as a motivation program are always short lived or nonexistent. Should we throw out programs that can be abused? I submit that we would be left with no quality programs.

Triad Theorem 6: Managers, who work in the direction circle, need to understand the application of TQM programs in the other two circles.

While I was working at McDonnell Aircraft Corporation (MAC) in the mid-1960s, now McDonnell-Douglas Corporation, ZD was installed as the company goal. At that time it was the popular quality program in the defense industry. If a company had a contract with the government, it was expected to participate. MAC was a prime contractor for the Mercury and Gemini space capsule programs and builder of the F-4 Phantom jet fighter. We were all asked to sign a MAC employee ZD pledge to do our best work (What had we been doing?); motivational speeches were given by upper management; and we all received a ZD key ring. The key ring lasted longer than the ZD quality effort. I can still remember some of the discussions in our work group concerning ZD, and they weren't about how we could improve on quality.

ZD Abused in the Systems Circle. When ZD is applied to the output of a process, it's too late to be concerned about the quality of a product or service. This end-product emphasis, instead of process emphasis, causes actions that do not eliminate nonconformances and, in fact, usually degrade the performance of the process. Actions creating inferior results could be adding more inspection activities, inspecting larger samples or 100 percent of the output, and relying on machine tools that measure the last product and self-adjust to compensate for variation from target.

It takes leadership to turn a slogan into a meaningful statement. Good intentions won't do it—it takes hard work and responsible actions. So the ultimate outcome of a ZD program is management's responsibility. The decision coming out of the direction circle will determine whether the staff treats it as a motivation or a continuous improvement tool. ZD applied as a standard and facilitated by knowledgeable quality professionals in the systems circle drives continuous improvement. If there are defects present, improvement actions might include the application of statistical process control (SPC), eliminating special causes, and reducing the influence of common causes to gain a higher level of process capability and fewer or zero defects. Another action could be the formation of a CQI project team assigned to improve the system and/or process.

Do *What* Right the First Time? How does the TQM triad accept Peters' quote about doing it right the first time as being a dumb statement? Within the context of the direction circle, where Peters is usually standing, he is exactly right. To provide direction that will drive growth requires innovative ideas, and it's hard to be very innovative if you are worried about always making the right decisions. As stated previously, activities in this component can have some rather high risks attached to them. Business strategies about which markets to enter, what products to produce, and how to offer the ultimate in customer satisfaction won't always be right in an innovative organization, but this organization will be far better off than the timid one always attempting to do strategies right the first time. Therefore, many of Peters' comments are true within the context of the direction or people circles, but are false and completely out of context in the systems circle.

Triad Theorem 7: What may be true or acceptable in one circle may be false or unacceptable in another circle.

None of us would disagree that we want the pilot of our airplane to have a do-it-right-the-first-time attitude. On the other hand, the CEO of the airline should be taking risks and not attempting to pursue zero defects when developing strategies that will move the organization to the top among competitors. In the case of the CEO, the standard truly would be a "candidate for dumbest statement" (Peters 1995).

When it comes to doing things right the first time, the CEO and upper management do have a special responsibility concerning the organization's processes that are already in place.

Doing the Right Things. Russell Ackoff, author of *The Democratic Corporation,* in an address at the 1995 Iowa Excellence Forum, challenged the audience to question the value of eliminating defects. It could be an attempt at doing the wrong things right if the process that is producing defects is not an essential process. The elimination of nonessential processes must be addressed in the direction circle by management. If we are operating a process that is not worth doing at all, it would be a waste of time to support and pay for a CQI team to eliminate defects from the process. Doing so would be an example of the ineffective actions and results that can occur when TQM is practiced as no more than a continuous improvement process. Instead, in this case, management should be working on eliminating or reengineering the process.

The processes to then make sure we do the right things right reside in the systems circle and to some extent in the people circle. The CQI process is the major contributor in the systems circle to the assurance that the right things are done right, frequently with a strong secondary effect in the people circle.

The decisions on what are the right things to do are as important to the TQM initiative as to the operational processes.

All quality programs that an organization is planning to implement or that are presently operating in the people and systems circles rely on management in the direction circle to ensure that the activity is a required part of the organization's overall TQM plan. As a manager, how do you know what the right things are? Eileen Shapiro (1995, 181) gives some guidance: "Approach TQM as an iterative process, one in which you learn what others have done, make changes in your own organization, learn as you go, correct course, and make more changes." This approach of constantly evolving your organization's TQM system is supported and facilitated by the framework defined in the unified total quality model.

Cost of Quality—It's Not for Cost Reduction

A second example of a misunderstanding that can be corrected with the use of the TQM triad relates to the cost of quality. William Latzko and David Saunders (1995), in their book *Four Days with Dr. Deming,* discuss an example of the cost of quality being used as a management decision tool for cost reduction. (The cost-of-quality tool is defined in chapter 5, and an example is given in chapter 7.) A short-term quality cost reduction was produced by drastically reducing expenditures relating to the prevention and appraisal costs of quality, although no data were present to indicate that this move was appropriate. Two examples of this cost-cutting strategy are reducing the quality department staff size (prevention cost) and eliminating inspection steps in production processes (appraisal cost). These cost reductions resulted in a noticeable erosion of customer service, which in turn resulted in a large account being lost. The point was made that this methodology for cost reduction does not consider the unknown and unknowable costs.

An even more basic point that could be made is that a very powerful tool, the cost of quality, was misused by management. Managers can see general levels of costs related to poor quality in companywide cost-of-quality charts, and they might see trends, but there is not enough detail to make decisions about either choosing specific improvement projects or taking specific action to reduce certain costs. This makes the time spent collecting, collating, and presenting these general data a questionable quality-related exercise and expense.

Specific cost-of-quality information for improvement projects, on the other hand, is an excellent method of prioritizing, monitoring, and documenting results. Cost of quality is not a cost reduction methodology—it's a measure of the effectiveness of cost reduction methodologies. The cost-of-quality tool belongs in the systems circle, not the direction circle, with a secondary use as a communicating tool between teams and management.

Triad Theorem 8: Using a program in the wrong circle can be hazardous to an organization's health.

A third example of misunderstandings caused because of a lack of a unifying model involves the controversy surrounding reengineering, TQM, and CQI. This controversy may have caused more damage to the total quality movement than any other. Proponents of each methodology sometimes seem to be spending their energy on positioning their favorite program as "king of the quality mountain." In fact, the two methodologies of reengineering and CQI are strong partners in building an organization's TQM system. A side issue is the restrictive definition assigned to TQM by the proponents of reengineering. They define TQM by using a CQI definition, so practically every comparison then made is between TQM and reengineering, when the comparison should be between reengineering and CQI. As an example, Hammer and Stanton (1995, 97) state that "TQM stresses incremental improvement through structured problem solving." If the definition for TQM is expanded to reflect the umbrella nature illustrated by the TQM triad, both CQI and reengineering can then be accepted as uniquely different and valuable business management approaches within TQM.

As stated in chapter 2, CQI is a quality program for the systems circle and reengineering is a program for the direction circle. My reasons for placing reengineering in the direction circle will be defended in chapter 4; for now, trust me on this. Portraying both of the programs as pieces of the TQM puzzle eliminates the controversy that presently exists.

Triad Theorem 9: A program in one circle does not replace a program in another circle; they synergistically work together.

A fourth and final example relates to what Brown, Hitchcock, and Willard (1994, 60) address as "emphasizing courtesy instead of competence." The true root cause may not be a lack of employee competence in their jobs, but a lack of competence in systems-circle TQM methodologies. This is characterized, in the symbolism of the triad, as excessive emphasis placed on the people circle by some trainers at the expense of the systems circle. Organizations practicing this emphasis can be recognized by their poorly designed processes that are incapable of producing defect-free output, operated by very courteous employees. As a customer, you may not be satisfied with your purchase of a product or service, but their reaction to your dissatisfaction was "world-class quality."

Why does it seem that so many organizations do this? First, in the short term, it's less expensive. No need to train the staff in problem-solving techniques, the use of statistical tools, or how to flowchart their processes. Just show the staff a good customer service–attitude video and send them back to the unsuspecting customer. Certainly, in the long term this is disastrous for the organization, but it just proves to the myopic management that this TQM stuff wasn't going to work anyhow. Second, there are too many pseudoexperts offering people-circle training who believe poor service quality is usually a people problem. Third, this approach reinforces the traditional management philosophy that the staff, if properly trained, should be able to get it right. These managers and pseudoexperts evidently slept through Deming's (1986, 315) statement that 94 percent of the possibilities for improvement belong to the system and are, therefore, management's responsibility.

**Triad Theorem 10: Quality program activities
in the three triad circles must be balanced.**

Other examples of misunderstandings occur because of some
of the following reasons.

1. A strong belief in the methodologies of one circle, to
   the point of excluding programs that don't fit that
   circle. For example, the real profits come from management making the right decisions; this team stuff is a
   waste of time.
2. A fear of the unknown in another circle, turned into a
   rationalization that it's not important. This is especially
   true with the treatment of statistics-based methodologies by people-circle trainers.

In the past, we have downplayed, discarded, or ignored quality programs because of the misunderstanding caused by not
having a unified model that would accept all the quality programs. Organizations guided by biased or self-serving quality
leaders jumped from program to program, with no comprehen-
sive plan. We need to change the paradigm and begin to assem-
ble the TQM puzzle, not pick up a piece, fumble with it for a
year, and throw it away for a new piece. Hopefully, the preceding
examples illustrate the benefits of a unified approach to TQM.

Finally, contrived disagreements, simply to position one's
favorite program as better than another, do extreme damage to
the quality movement. Wouldn't it be more beneficial to position programs in a unified model and illustrate how they all synergistically work together?

Management Fad of the Year

We've probably all experienced or observed organizations moving from one quality program to another like so many stepping-
stones across a stream. The metaphor is not apt, since a quality
program should not be used for a period of time and then discarded for another if an organization expects to reach full im-

plementation of TQM. In addition, the philosophy of TQM as a rewarding, never-ending journey, not a final destination of full implementation, is missed by these organizations. Instead of a continuously evolving process of adding elements to a TQM system, the appearance is that of wandering through quality program after quality program — more like total quality chaos than total quality management.

Much of this chaos is generated by upper management's failure to grasp the TQM concepts and manage their implementation wisely. Of course, they don't get much help from the purveyors of TQM "panacea" programs. Shapiro (1995, xvii) in addressing fads and panaceas stresses "the need for the courage to manage: to assess situations, set an overall course or focus, think through options, develop plans, take action, modify plans, learn and go forward... this courage is more valuable than ever." The courage to manage the TQM initiative is based on knowledge, and the foundation for the knowledge can be the unified total quality model.

Management must develop the ability to create TQM solutions customized for the company's particular needs. The TQM triad provides a template for a unified approach to designing a unique TQM system. With a model in hand that consolidates but allows for diversity, the activities that create fads are eliminated.

The Search for the Golden Panacea

An activity that could be considered the root cause of fad creation is the search for the panacea program. The next quality program brought into the company — and it's usually considered a replacement program — has been introduced with the fervor and fanfare of a panacea. The previous quality program, now or soon to be relegated to fad status, had the same introduction a year or two ago. Today's panacea becomes tomorrow's fad. This has nothing to do with the ability or potential of any quality program to produce its stated objectives, but everything to do with weak assimilation. By weak assimilation, I'm referring to the propensity of an organization to spend resources on training and implementing a quality program, practice the methodologies for a period of time (approximately one to three years), gain positive results (although many times unmeasured and undocumented), and toss it all away for the next quality program. Time after time, organizations have turned their backs on everything they've invested in implementing a quality program because some new program was being promoted in the popular press as the wave of the future in business management.

Continually changing quality programs causes negative reactions in the workforce that are far reaching, deep, and long lived. No matter how much the new program looks like the panacea of panaceas, to the workers out there in the trenches who have been trying to keep up with the training for these new management fads, it's just another in a seemingly never-ending series of futile attempts.

Examples of this behavior are too easy to find. The following real-life scenario illustrates the panacea-to-fad syndrome. After recounting this story, I'll revisit it using the TQM triad to model a unified approach to arrive at a different outcome.

Implementing Quality Programs Without the TQM Triad

A manufacturing company of approximately 2500 employees, T. Q. Manufacturing (a fictitious name), started its quality efforts in the early 1980s. The first program to be implemented was a quality circles approach, the hot business management topic of that era. Approximately half of the workforce, those directly related with manufacturing and assembly, received two days' training in problem solving with a team approach. The support staff—sales, marketing, design engineering, accounting, testing, and payroll—were not included because the perception was that quality circles were for the shop. This effort continued for approximately three years, with some good results from machining and assembly teams. With changes in management, diminishing results, and resultant lack of support, the quality circle program was allowed to fade.

Quality program number two was a fresh start in 1985. This time the main effort was with the support staff. Approximately 1200 staff members received 20 hours of training in a quality improvement process, and the shop workers received 4 hours of awareness training. This training was customer focused and based in team problem solving. Quality improvement teams were formed at all company sites and guided by a steering committee. The call went out for problems to eliminate, corrective action forms were collected, and a flurry of activity took place. Once again there were some good results, and once again the process began to fade. The shop workers had now been hit with two large and disjointed doses of training in the name of quality.

Quality program number three was another fresh start in the early 1990s. This time the effort was again focused on the support staff, and specifically on those that had direct contact with the final customer. The theme of this activity seemed to be customer satisfaction at all costs. Manufacturing-related actions that were necessitated by this customer focus were not supported by an internal quality improvement process because it had been allowed to fade away. The shop had to rely on expensive quick fixes to satisfy the customer.

Without the structure of a model like the TQM triad and with only the guidance of the purveyors of the quality programs, the end result should not come as a surprise. Serial implementation of seemingly disjointed quality programs, with no vision of them being integrated into a total quality system, produces in the final analysis nothing more than a frustrated workforce and a trail of expensive training programs.

Using the TQM Triad to Implement Quality Programs

What could the unified total quality model approach look like for this scenario? First, here are some of the principles behind the TQM triad that will influence the decisions concerning new quality program implementation.

1. The TQM triad emphasizes the need for concurrent, integrated, and logically ordered quality programs.

2. Combining, blending, and building on existing quality processes with new quality programs produces added dividends of synergy and eliminates fad thinking.

Following is one possible TQM triad–influenced scenario. An underlying change would be the integration of the diverse quality programs based on the just-listed two principles. Each sequential quality program would not have been allowed to fade away because of the necessity of integrating them and building on them with the latest quality program to create a viable TQM system.

The introduction of the second program would now be implemented within the context of the existing quality circle process already functioning in the shop. A kick-off discussion with both the shop workers and support staff would address the placement of the new quality program in the systems circle and its blending with the quality circle process. It would be presented as the next element of the growing TQM system being added to the organization, bringing increased effectiveness and customer focus. A comparison of the quality circle problem-solving approach (program one) to the quality improvement team problem-solving approach (program two) indicates that the first is a more rigorous procedure. Therefore, the shop workers would not be retrained in a new problem-solving process, but would continue to use the quality circle approach with which they were already familiar.

The following topics would be covered in the shop training for introduction of the second program. The shop workers would receive more than just the awareness training session they received in the first scenario. They would study

1. Defining quality in terms of the customers' requirements
2. Internal and external customers
3. Quality improvement methodologies
4. Integrating quality circles, quality improvement teams, and the steering committee

The support staff would receive the same training for the second quality program they had received in the first scenario, with one change. The problem-solving procedure would be replaced by the procedure from the original quality circle training utilized in the shop. This would allow for easier facilitation of cross-functional teams made up of members from the shop and staff. Also, an explanation of the quality circle history at the company would be included in the staff training.

At this point, the first two quality programs would be integrated. The shop workers, already old hands with quality circle teams, would perceive this latest move by management as one of building on past successes. It wouldn't be the practice of "that didn't work, let's try something new," with the outcome of the quality circle approach turning into a fad.

Now along comes program three, the customer satisfaction improvement process. This new program would be positioned in the people circle to work concurrently and synergistically with the existing quality improvement processes in the systems circle. It would be explained that this addition to the TQM system would strengthen the customer focus and provide the internal quality improvement process with new direction. The training would be basically the same as the first scenario, with the addition of an awareness session for the shop workers. In the triad-influenced scenario, however, it would not be customer satisfaction at all costs, with one quick fix after another. When the customer satisfaction improvement process indicates that a problem exists, there would now be a supporting internal quality improvement process that would drive the required corrective actions.

Why were programs one and two still in place in the TQM triad scenario when program three came along? Because program one was not allowed to fade but was combined with program two. Integrating the quality programs will send a strong signal: We are building something here, not just trying one management fad after another. Having accomplished this triad-driven action one time reinforces the long-term view of TQM and makes the next program introduction just that much easier.

What was an organization-shocking change is now a comfortable evolution when new quality programs are added.

Is It Too Late?

One might argue that this example comparison of TQM implementation, without and then with the triad, is an exercise in Monday morning quarterbacking and the problem can't really be solved for this company. That's correct when looking at past history, but the saga continues both for this company and for all others. It's not too late to eliminate the next disjointed attempt at implementing a quality program.

As a CEO or member of upper management, how can you introduce a new quality program and avoid the fad trap? You can

1. Place the new program—that is, identify its circle—within the context of the unified total quality model.
2. Indicate the reason for the additional quality program.
3. Discuss how this program will blend with other programs already implemented in this and the other two circles.
4. Eliminate redundant activities in the new program that already are present in previously implemented programs.
5. Continue to support the entire TQM effort—not just the latest program.

 **Chapter 4**

The Direction Circle

Introduction

The next three chapters have as one objective the differentiation of the three circles of the unified total quality model. This will be accomplished by (1) delineating attributes that help define each circle and (2) discussing representative tools, activities, and methodologies that reside in each of the circles. These actions will provide guidelines for the placement of quality programs in their correct circle; in addition, the discussion of well-known quality programs and where they fit in the model further differentiates the three circles. Hopefully, this will give you a guide to follow when adding your own favorite quality programs to the list. Reengineering and continuous quality improvement will be strongly emphasized in this discussion for two reasons: They are perhaps the best known methodologies, and they reside in different circles. The first reason allows for more easily understood examples, explanations, and comparisons. Understanding the second reason assists in differentiating two of the circles.

We shall start the tour around the TQM triad at the direction circle. It's positioned at the bottom of the TQM triad (see Figure 4.1) for good reason. Managers, the occupants of this circle, are not pictured at the top of the hierarchical pyramid, but at the foundation of the organization's TQM efforts. They

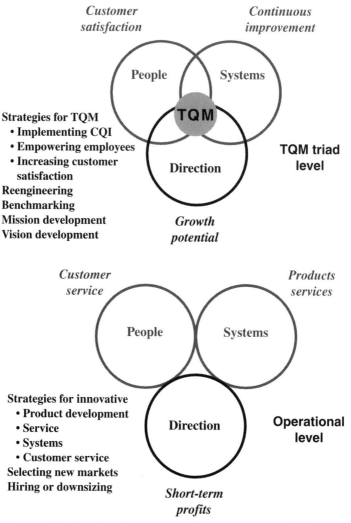

Figure 4.1: *The direction circles at the operational and TQM triad levels.*

initiate the strategies that drive the other two circles, both at the operational and TQM levels.

Developing Strategies—A Prime Attribute

The strategies that cause innovations in products, services, and systems are grounded in the direction circle at the operational level, and all TQM strategies start in the direction circle at the TQM triad level. Whether the strategy is implementing CQI, empowering employees, or reengineering a major business process, the decision to do it comes from this circle. Some decisions are for actions within the direction circle—developing a mission statement or reengineering—while others are decisions that affect the other two circles, such as CQI and employee empowerment.

So there are two necessary aspects to the direction circle. The first is directing the organization's innovation and offering of products and services (operational level), while the second is directing the TQM effort (TQM triad level). At both levels the transformation of direction—that is, strategies—into organizational change requires interaction, usually communication, with People and Systems (see Figure 4.2). The directing or interaction attribute sets the direction circle apart from the other two circles and is consistent with placing management here. Management communicates the vision and mission throughout the organization. Management communicates why the organization is implementing a new piece of the TQM system— for example, SPC, customer surveys, or continuous quality improvement. This should not be a one-time act of communi-

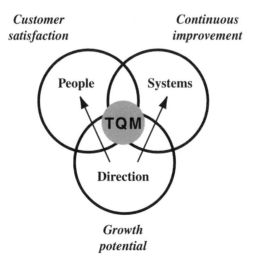

Figure 4.2: *Direction circle strategies drive people-circle and systems-circle actions.*

cation—it's ongoing, day in and day out. What would an organization's profits look like if the CEO communicated the goals at the start of the fiscal year and then did nothing more all year long? This need for ongoing communication and management of the TQM processes can be threatening for CEOs or any upper managers. Their training and understanding is still new to them—as new as it is to the people they're expected to lead.

Attributes of the Direction Circle — Placement Criteria

The focus of the following attribute discussion will be on the TQM triad level. Characteristics or attributes of the direction circle will assist in the assignment of certain tools, activities, and methodologies to this section of the TQM triad. The following attributes (placement criteria) are associated with this circle: high risk, rapid response, growth potential, and management driven. A candidate program for this circle doesn't have to possess all of these attributes, just one or more.

High Risk

An attribute of all quality programs is the risk involved in not getting an expected or hoped-for outcome. The level of risk can be a determinant in the positioning of a quality program in the TQM triad. Therefore, when attempting to position a new program within the triad, make a judgment on risk potential. Many activities residing in and strategies coming out of the direction circle have the inherent characteristic of high risk. This is consistent with their assignment to the managers' circle. The demands and responsibilities for making high-risk decisions certainly go with the management job description.

Continuous improvement and customer satisfaction are the stated outcomes for the systems and people circles, respectively. Why is the outcome of the direction circle stated as growth potential, instead of organizational growth? The use of the word *potential* reflects the high risk that is present in this circle, where successful results are not ensured. Even the decisions required in the direction circle at the operational level—those of deciding direction for innovative products, customer services, and business processes—carry with them high risk. Organizational growth, measured as either an incremental or dramatic increase, is not a guaranteed outcome of actions taken in this circle. On the other hand, actions taken in the systems and people circles will practically always net increases respectively in continuous improvement and customer satisfaction, some small and some large.

One of the more popular methodologies that has this high-risk attribute is reengineering. Hammer and Stanton (1995, 45, 46) acknowledge the need to take risks while reengineering: "A willingness to fail is a prerequisite for significant success" and "risk is acceptable and to be tolerated." They indicate that reengineering is very difficult, and 50 percent to 70 percent of the attempts were not successful in meeting expectations.

One consultant, Elizabeth D. Johnson (1994, 8), has observed measurable improvements but still states, "Re-engineering is disruptive, expensive, traumatic for staff and management, and offers no up-front guarantee of real improvement."

Developing the strategies for an organization's CQI efforts, a direction-circle activity, also contains elements of high risk. Discussions about CQI failure always seem to focus on strategic issues—for instance, lack of management commitment. One never hears of a fully implemented CQI process being disruptive, traumatic, or not producing at least some continuous improvement. Yes, you may hear complaints about the expense, but that's due to lack of cost-of-quality information. We'll take that issue up later. Once CQI has been installed as a systems-circle methodology, the actual process of continuous improvement is fairly low risk and does not contain the implementation or operational problems inherent in reengineering.

Activities are also assigned to this circle that do not have high risk attached, such as developing a mission statement, establishing a vision, or increasing the focus on customer service. These activities can usually be identified as having one or more of the following attributes associated with the direction circle.

Rapid Response

Being able to respond rapidly to changes in the organization's operating environment, whether a hospital responding to rapid health care changes or a computer manufacturer responding to technological changes, is an important direction-circle attribute. The strategic guidance emanating from the direction circle concerning CQI implementation, customer satisfaction improvement, and reengineering application is more effective when exhibiting this attribute.

A Department of Veterans Affairs Medical Center's actions illustrate this attribute. Hospital management, sensing a need to shift to outpatient surgery, immediately directed a reengineering effort to redesign the necessary supporting business processes. As patients and medical staff identified problems with the new outpatient surgery processes, a CQI team was made available to formulate corrective actions.

This attribute can become a double-edged sword. The wrong type of rapid response action in this circle harms the efforts in the other two circles that are continuous and long-term activities. The negative scenario: General Marketing is moving through the early difficult implementation phase of its quality process started two years ago. Training continues, and project teams are starting to show success. The CEO reads an article in the Sunday business section of the local newspaper highlighting Premium Manufacturing's great success with a new quality management methodology. On Monday morning, General Marketing is going to suffer a deadly course change in its TQM efforts. The sad thing is that many of these jumps are to methodologies that are very similar in activities and outcomes—just new buzzword names.

Growth Potential

This attribute is also the outcome resulting from actions taken in the direction circle at the TQM triad level. It could certainly be thought of as belonging with each circle, but in the direction circle it is the primary result. A CQI project team (located in the systems circle) that develops a breakthrough in a major business system may document a decrease in product cost, an increase in product quality levels, and/or faster deliveries to the customer. All these results in the systems circle lead to the secondary result of growth potential for the organization.

Back in the direction circle, the primary reason for deciding to implement one of the resident activities or programs is the promise of growth potential. The problems start when growth potential and short-term profits are equated or interchanged. If management focuses only on the output at the operational level (short-term profits), believing that if managers' actions are planned based on the short-term profit aspect the organizational growth will automatically follow, they are probably setting themselves up for long-term disappointment—if not for themselves, at least for the company's stockholders. To gain the benefits of the TQM system, management must move its attention to the triad level and focus on those activities that yield the outcome of growth potential.

A CEO elects to implement the TQM strategy of employee empowerment, an action to strengthen the people circle. If the reason for this action is short-term profits, one would have to wonder if the action would even be contemplated. The connection between employee empowerment and growth potential does seem plausible, however. The CEO might reason that empowered employees would be more creative, accept ownership of their work processes, and become more customer focused—certainly all characteristics that could effect growth potential, but probably not effect short-term profits.

At the macro level, where management is operating, implementation of an employee empowerment program is for the payoff of organizational growth potential. At the micro level, what the staff sees in the people circle are the advantages of employee empowerment as related to customer satisfaction. If employees begin to self-manage their processes, they will be redesigning them to more efficiently meet the internal and external customers' needs. The big picture of organizational growth is left for management to pursue.

The preceding discussion related to the importance of management decisions based on the growth potential possible from

TQM strategies. There does need to be a balance with strategies focused on short-term profits. An organization that becomes entirely absorbed with TQM programs can lose sight of operational-level issues. Neglecting to plan for new products, services, and markets can cause an organization to get into trouble with quality program implementations in other circles. If a company is experiencing success with CQI teams (systems circle) but fails to make the right decisions related to new product development, it can loose market share even with the best product quality and customer service quality. Some might mistakenly label this a failure of CQI when, in fact, it's just the garden-variety business problem of zigging when they should have zagged. TQM does not come with a crystal ball.

Management Driven, Directed, or Owned

The strategies deriving from the direction circle and leading the actions by individuals and teams are management driven, not customer driven. Innovation is way ahead of the customer — customers aren't even aware that they need the product or service in many cases. What customer demanded a CD-ROM, Pentium processor, or microwave oven? What customer demanded that the company start a CQI process? After these products have been introduced to the marketplace or the quality improvement process has started, the focus better be on the customer — management driven, customer focused.

You may have heard that TQM, or any of its constituent programs, is a new way of managing. The context is often that of "discard your present methodologies and switch to TQM." In fact, these quality-related management programs are a new level superimposed on an organization's existing management practices. The existing practices are in the direction circle at the operational level. The quality-related programs are present in the TQM triad level direction circle. This construction, of course, assumes that the management practices already in place are capable of supporting the TQM system. If an organization is in need of a major reengineering of its management practices, attempting to implement TQM may be like applying a new coat of paint to a car that is rusting out from the inside—it looks good for now, but it won't last. Quality outcomes ensue as effective interactions develop between existing good management practices and TQM triad level processes.

Does this mean managers have even more to do as a TQM system is developed in their organizations? Yes, in the short term; and then as the quality processes start netting results and employees are empowered to improve their processes, managers' jobs should become more hassle-free.

Quality "Controlled" Without a TQM System. The ultimate problem is attempting a quality revolution without a management-driven TQM system—managements' failure to make the leap of faith to the TQM triad level. But quality cannot be dispersed throughout the operational-level processes without the TQM methodologies resident in the TQM triad level.

Take a look at attempts at quality using the traditional management of the operational level. Products are being shipped with nonconformances, customer complaints grow, and management descends on the problem: the quality control department. If they are going to be called quality control, why can't they control quality? It's clear to see that they are overwhelmed with work; adding more inspectors should fix the problem. Customer complaints remain high and are trending higher, product returns are increasing, and more rejects are being found by the expanded inspection staff. At this time the company invests in a massive customer service effort. A new process and associated support system are designed to provide the unhappy customers with a method for easy return of defective products. The company continues its quality actions by downsizing to keep the profits up.

One could say that this scenario is certainly management driven, but the management team did not leave the comforting confines of the direction circle at the operational level. Every activity was a traditional management technique that in the short term may produce profits—but without interaction from the TQM level, this organization is doomed. In this case the interaction is usually missing because there is no TQM level.

That First TQM Success Was the Last. Another problem that is expensive and at the same time crippling to an organization's future quality efforts is that of installing a beautifully designed quality program but not being able to gain improvements in the operational-level processes. This differs from the first scenario where no viable TQM triad level even existed. Now one exists, but it remains detached and unproductive relative to the "real" business at the operational level. This second scenario is played out in far too many organizations. In fact, it happens so frequently—and does exhibit seemingly positive results— that it sometimes is mistakenly identified as a TQM success. Possible root causes are (1) management thinking that quality programs can be purchased off the shelf and installed by a quality consultant and (2) management believing its role is to select a responsible TQM head, supply the person with resources, and support the TQM effort with rhetoric. What develops is a phenomenon I've labeled a *quality nova*.

The players in this quality program implementation are usually an outside consultant or trainer, the management steering committee, a responsible TQM head, and a couple project teams. This scenario starts innocently enough, with the choice of a trainer or consultant and his or her quality improvement training package. (By the way, this has nothing to do with the caliber of the material or the trainer.) Training ensues with a couple of selected project teams. These teams are facilitated by the outside trainer and are practically guaranteed to produce success stories, partially to validate the organization's expense for the training and partially to prove that the quality improvement methodology does, in fact, work in this organization's "unique" type of business. It seems that the common knowledge is, we are different, are you sure this TQM stuff will work in our business?

Outside trainers or consultants will make sure the teams are successful because they are being paid for that outcome and they take their responsibility seriously. The initial teams present their completed projects to the impressed management steering committee who now seems ready to take over the process. This is where the baton seems to be dropped. A good process has been installed at the TQM level and has been demonstrated by the installer, but the organization can't repeat the early successes. The steering committee continues to support the TQM process by establishing CQI project teams, providing meeting resources, and reviewing results. Whenever someone is asked about the organization's TQM success, however, the initial projects are always marched out as the proof. The label *quality nova* derives from the sudden burst of activity followed by a gradual fading to its former intensity, just like a nova in the heavens. This decline continues for two or three years until a new buzzword program attracts management's interest, then we're off on a new crusade.

What happened? Management drove the formation of the TQM level, but did not continue by driving the linkage of the TQM level with the operational level. This linkage action blends the TQM effort into the normal work of the business, instead of isolating it as a separate unique practice. TQM, oh yeah, that's what we do every Tuesday at 10:00 A.M.

Tools, Activities, and Methodologies

What are some of the tools, activities, and methodologies that exhibit the previously defined attributes and, therefore, should be assigned to the direction circle? I'll list a few in each category, and you can add your own favorites. When the new quality programs come along, and they most certainly will, add them too.

Tools

Management has the largest selection of tools available for use, including the seven basic tools of quality, the seven management and planning tools, and the cost of quality. These tools work equally as well at both the TQM triad and operational levels. If a manager is reengineering a business process, the tools will be required, and when he or she is managing business processes, the tools are an effective aid. The cost of quality will be discussed in chapter 7 as one of the primary communication tools between the systems and direction circles.

The Seven Basic Tools of Quality. These are a collection of powerful tools for process analysis, data analysis, systems design, and problem solution. The list includes the flowchart, Pareto chart, cause-and-effect diagram, histogram, run chart, scatter diagram, and control chart. Applications for these tools exist in all three circles; therefore all potential users, whether individuals, teams, or managers, need to be conversant in their utilization. In other words, a prerequisite to building a viable TQM system is that every person in the organization be able to successfully wield the seven basic tools of quality.

The reader may be inclined to place the seven basic tools in the systems circle. After all, aren't these the tools used by the CQI teams? An organization that doesn't also make use of the seven basic tools in the people and direction circles is missing a tremendous opportunity for building process knowledge and increasing the effectiveness of decision-making processes.

Control charts in the direction circle. Knowledge gained by realizing how variation is affecting the process you are managing or operating is one reward for understanding and using the seven basic tools, specifically the control charts. Deming (1993, 96) felt this important enough to include "knowledge about variation" as one of the four parts of his system of profound knowledge. Understanding the effects of variation and being able to identify common and special causes of process variation is fundamental to operation, management, and improvement of processes in all three triad circles.

Arguably one of the biggest flaws with many organizations' TQM systems is the lack of control chart usage by management. Management, and everyone in the organization, loses on two counts. First, management should be modeling all facets of the TQM effort; and second, important knowledge is gained from processes by using these statistical tools.

Why don't managers appreciate the usefulness of control charts? One explanation could be their perception that managing by the numbers is really an art learned through experience. It turns out that the reason it seems to be an art and not a science is exactly the same reason that statistical tools are needed in the management process—process variation.

New and inexperienced managers come to their positions expecting to make prescient decisions based on the numbers their staffs provide. They discover that there appears to be no such thing as hard facts when it comes to managing their organizations' output, sales, and expenses. A number is compared to the same measure from last month, last quarter, and/or a year ago, and using that "insight" a management decision is reached. It seems that half the time they are wrong—management by the numbers, therefore, must be an art. In fact, what has hindered the manager attempting to gain knowledge from a piece of business process data is the lack of ability to separate process signals from process noise. Understanding process variation becomes the key to gaining the ability to tell the difference between noise and signal. This understanding develops from the knowledge gained by using control charts to analyze business process data.

Managers in the direction circle lead implementation. Managers can start the practice of using the seven basic tools for the entire organization. Modeling the usage of the tools allows managers to become conversant with them while employing the tools as communicators of information between the circles. As managers become enlightened as to the efficiency of these basic tools as communicators of information, they will start to request their application in reports and presentations. What better way to drive the utilization of the seven basic tools of quality in the people and systems circles?

As managers' comfort levels increase with the seven basic tools, they will soon discover that their own processes benefit from application of the tools, as has already been noted with control charts. An appreciation for the variation present in management data—whether related to sales, production, quality, shipments, or any other process they monitor—will translate into enthusiastic implementation and continued use of SPC techniques. They will begin to speak of their processes in terms of common and special causes of variation and will take appropriate management action based on this knowledge. No longer will managers do what could be labeled as single point management—the act of making decisions based on the last monthly or quarterly data point.

Two secondary effects will be noted as managers become more practiced in using control charts in data analysis. (1) There will be a move away from the dependence on reams of computer printouts to run the business. Instead, selected charts will display business process information including the process capability and signals indicating the likely presence of special causes of variation. (2) The understanding that some special-cause detection rules require the observation of more than one data point (for example, one signal that indicates the likely presence of a process shift requires eight points on one side of the centerline of the control chart) will prompt management to begin looking at measurements weekly or even daily instead of the past standard frequency of monthly or quarterly.

The Seven Management and Planning Tools. The other list of seven tools, labeled the seven management and planning tools (7 MP), will be assigned to the direction circle based on the guidance offered by Michael Brassard (1989, 9) in *The Memory Jogger Plus+™*. Brassard states, "The 7 MP [management and planning] Tools have proven useful to managers of virtually any level in a company. However, they have proven to be particularly helpful for middle to upper managers." It could be argued that the 7 MP tools are also effective in the other two circles, but it's advisable for an organization to become proficient in the seven basic tools of quality first. Expecting everyone in the organization to become proficient in 14 tools is probably an unnecessary requirement.

The 7 MP tools are the following:

1. Affinity diagram
2. Interrelationship digraph
3. Tree diagram
4. Prioritization matrices
5. Matrix diagram
6. Process decision program chart
7. Activity network diagram

I refer the interested reader to Brassard's book for guidance in the use of the 7 MP tools.

Activities

This classification usually consists of singular actions by management that produce desired outcomes related to the TQM system. Much of the Direction output that interacts with People and Systems (see Figure 4.1) is produced by activities—many of which cause processes to start up, define new processes, or provide guidance for staff members and teams. Example activities that fit here are

1. Developing a mission statement
2. Developing an organizational vision
3. Initiating implementation of CQI
4. Developing employee empowerment strategies

Each activity provides strategical information for the rest of the triad. The output of the first two activities, a mission and a vision, would be communicated to the entire organization after completion by management. Activity 3 would be an interaction between the direction and systems circles, while activity 4 represents an interaction between the direction and people circles.

Methodologies

These systems of methods, principles, and rules for a given discipline are the procedures that contribute a high proportion of the Direction outcome, growth potential. One important use of the seven basic tools is as fundamental elements in these methodologies. In addition, activities—such as developing a vision—can drive the use of certain methodologies like reengineering and benchmarking.

Reengineering. This is a prominent methodology in the direction circle. This placement of reengineering is based on the definition and approach as presented by Hammer and Champy (1993, 32) Their definition follows.

> *Reengineering:* The fundamental rethinking and radical redesign of business processes to achieve dramatic improvements in critical, contemporary measures of performance, such as cost, quality, service, and speed.

Key words in this definition provide the reasons for assigning reengineering to the direction circle. Radical redesign of business processes, which can mean job changes or position elimination, requires strong leadership and participation from senior-level management. This reliance on management for a successful outcome meets the management directed and owned placement criteria for Direction. Radical redesign implies high risk, so reengineering also meets that criteria. In addition, reengineering certainly has a primary objective of generating growth potential for an organization.

We have all read about, and some of you may have personally experienced, organizations that use reengineering as a code word for downsizing. Does this mean the activity of downsizing is in this circle of the TQM triad level? No. Downsizing only produces short-term profits, so it is more realistically placed in Directions at the operational level. It is no more than a traditional, albeit poor, means of controlling operational expenses and is not part of the TQM system. Organizations that attempt to make downsizing part of TQM violate the following theorem.

Triad Theorem 11: An activity, tool, or methodology in one circle should not negate, contradict, or undermine an activity, tool, or methodology in another circle.

Downsizing has a deleterious effect on both Systems and People. It limits the ability of an organization to conduct CQI projects because of the resultant impact on resource availability, especially staff able to invest precious time in team meetings. If the workforce is stressed, it will not treat the customer in a way that will create delighted customers.

One last point about reengineering. If your definition, understanding, or practice of it would lead you to argue that it belongs in Systems, because it is no different than CQI in your organization, and examples certainly can be found, that's fine. The unified total quality model is flexible. If reengineering cannot be discerned from CQI in your organization, however, and you need to truly reinvent a business process, what methodology will you use?

It may be advisable to think of reengineering and CQI as opposite ends of a process improvement continuum, with one end anchored in the direction circle and the other in the systems circle. As one moves from reengineering to CQI on this continuum, the amount of management control changes. Upper management retains a high degree of control in reengineering, but in CQI, the teams are empowered to take control of business processes.

Benchmarking. Many attributes of reengineering are shared by benchmarking, therefore, this methodology will also be assigned to Direction.

> *Benchmarking:* The search for and the integration of
> business process best practices into an organization to
> create the potential for dramatic increases in performance.

Both approaches expect radical changes in business processes, strive for dramatic increases in performance, and employ similar activities. The starting points of the two methodologies become the defining difference. Reengineering starts with a blank sheet of paper, and benchmarking with identified best practices. Starting at seemingly opposite points also separates the two based on risk exposure. One outcome will be virtually a new, untested, innovative system, while the other has been pre-viously tested and refined by another organization to the point of being a recognized best practice. Since the radical changes and dramatic increases imply changes in processes, if not sys-tems, a high level of management participation is necessary.

Interaction of the TQM Triad and Operational Levels

The tools, activities, and methodologies of any triad-level circle can operate on processes in any other operational-level circle, but the primary interaction is between like circles—for example, the direction circle at the TQM triad level with the direction circle at the operational level (see Figure 4.3). Secondary interactions—those that involve different circles at each level or more compli-cated interrelationships—are no less important than the primary interactions and will be discussed in chapter 7. To simplify Fig-ure 4.3, the term *methodology* will be assumed to include the tools and activities that also reside in the direction circle.

Two examples follow that illustrate the cycle of interactions modeled by Figure 4.3. Starting at the top of the figure with growth potential methodologies, their interaction with opera-tional-level processes is the first step. An example growth po-tential methodology (an activity) would be the development of

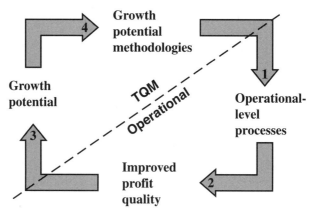

Figure 4.3: *The growth potential interaction cycle.*

a vision that drives an organization to thrive on innovative, bold experimentation à la Tom Peters—a place where risks are taken daily, and both successes and failures are celebrated. The environment created by this TQM activity improves the ability of the organization to create innovative products and services and to select new markets, both operational-level processes of the direction circle.

Improved profit quality, as defined in the operational definition example in the next section, results from the impact of the introduction of innovative products and services. One of the criteria for determining quality profits is that of having a percentage of the profits generated by innovative products and services.

This improvement in profit quality, caused by innovative products and services, in turn translates into growth potential for the organization. The process completes a full cycle when increased growth potential provides the impetus for the application of more growth potential methodologies.

Another example growth potential methodology (a tool) is SPC. As managers utilize the control charts to monitor processes and base their process management decisions on SPC-derived knowledge, the operational-level processes are positively affected. Operational-level processes that are statistically in control and exhibit reduced variability will improve the profit quality. The improvement stems from the continuous improvement aspect of using SPC and the increased customer satisfaction from products and services produced with less variability—that is, more consistent products and services. Once again, the improved profit quality generates growth potential, and the cycle is complete.

Before leaving this subject of interactions between the levels, there is one general class of them that should be mentioned. These interactions could be called management directives for the people and systems circles. It's probably fairly obvious that most activities and processes outside of the direction circle require an initial step by management in the direction circle to provide the resources and approval for start-up or continuation.

For example, the process of continuous quality improvement in the systems circle might be started with a directive from management. After the start-up, the cycle then works between the two levels of the systems circle (see chapter 5).

Measure of Success

The concept of measuring the success of individual quality program implementations and the TQM system as a whole requires an understanding of the two levels pictured in Figure 4.1. In general, the measures of success for the TQM-level processes are reflected in the improved quality of the outputs of the operational-level processes. Therefore, the measure of success for the TQM triad level direction circle is most directly measured by the improved quality of the short-term profits, the output of the direction circle at the operational level. Note that the measure of success is a differential comparison—not gauging a quality level, but gauging the improvement from a past quality level.

Process output of the operational-level direction circle is considered short-term profits, because long-term profits are just an extension over time of the profit trend generated by applying TQM principles and techniques. If the short-term profits do not meet the criteria of the following operational definition, long-term profits likely will not follow. A fundamental roadblock develops for effective TQM implementation when success is defined by the size, not the improved quality, of short-term profits.

If we want to ensure the success of quality program implementations leading to a TQM system, an operational definition for quality profits is needed. The concept of profit quality and the four-part model for an operational definition were introduced in chapter 2. Following is an example of an operational definition for quality profits.

1. *Define the characteristic to be measured.* The quality of the organization's short-term (monthly or quarterly) profits.
2. *Choose a measurement device.* The quality profit template: a questionnaire that audits and appraises the

TQM constituent processes that are operating to affect the profits of the organization.

3. *Describe the method for measurement.*
   a. Is there a cost-of-quality component to the profits derived from CQI activities in the systems circle? What is it in dollars?
   b. Is there both an internal and external customer satisfaction index? What is the CSI increase since last period?
   c. Is a percentage (to be determined by the organization) of the profits generated by innovative products, services, and systems (new to the organization in the last year)? What is the increase in profit in the last period due to innovation?
4. *State the decision criteria for evaluation of the resulting measurements.* Profits will be considered quality if the answers to the first questions in step 3a, 3b, and 3c are yes.

Why are quality profits important? Aren't all profit dollars the same? Organizations operating without a TQM system strive to maximize profits with no thought to the other components of the triad. Quality profit, as measured by the previous operational definition or one you might construct with the same format, includes contributions from each of the three triad circles. Questions 3a, 3b, and 3c correspond to the systems, people, and direction circles. Managers monitoring the implementation of the TQM system using the quality profit operational definition are ensured of taking into account effects from all three components of the triad. TQM gains its power from the three working in unison, all producing outputs and taking advantage of between-circle synergism.

A monthly or quarterly report based on the aggregate answer to the second questions in each of 3a, 3b, and 3c will indicate the level of improvement in quality profits, reflecting managements' success in generating growth potential. The profit-and-loss (P&L) statement will remain the ultimate measure of success for an organization, whether TQM is present or not.

With a TQM system in place, the improved quality of the profit line on the P&L statement is one method of documenting the success measure for the direction circle.

Triad Theorem 12: The measures of success of the TQM triad level processes are found in the improved quality performance of processes at the operational level.

Deming's 14 Points for Management

Much of Deming's focus was on the people that were responsible for transforming the organization—management. This philosophy is illustrated best by his 14 points for management (Deming 1986). They reside in this circle, providing management the basis to lead the efforts in the other two circles. These points for management can be categorized as the foundation for the TQM implementation effort. I will not rehash the 14 points as there are many fine books available that discuss them in detail, certainly the prime being Deming's own book, *Out of the Crisis.*

As managers adopt the 14 points and develop strategies based on a thorough understanding of them, the true TQM transformation begins. This singular action by management can be the agent that changes the quality programs being implemented from fads to valuable additions to the organization's method of conducting business. For example, in chapter 3, I stated that a root cause of fad creation is the search for the panacea program. One symptom of this root cause is the continual changing of quality programs. Deming's first point for management addresses the issue of constancy of purpose. Certainly an element of that would be not changing the direction of the organization's quality efforts with each new buzzword program that comes along. Constancy of purpose negates the activities that create fads out of viable quality programs. Building the TQM system with the TQM triad conveys a long-term unified approach—constancy of purpose.

Although the 14 points are primarily guidance for management in leading the TQM initiative, they do offer useful instructions for teams and individuals and, therefore, should be included in everyone's TQM training. For example, workers in the systems and people circles need to understand how to select suppliers and why inspection is not a good way to cause quality—both topics that are addressed in the 14 points.

 **Chapter 5**

The Systems Circle

Introduction

We continue our tour around the TQM triad with a stop at the systems circle. At the operational level, systems are producing the products and services that are the organization's reason for being. Work teams, whether traditional or self-directed, operate the bulk of the processes residing here. We are interested in the systems circle at the triad level, where actions are taken that transform operational systems through redesign or continuous improvement (see Figure 5.1). Certainly everyone—management, individuals, and teams—works daily with systems and processes. In this circle the focus is on analyzing and changing these systems and processes using the methodologies of TQM and the power of cross-functional teams.

Processes and Systems—What's the Difference?

Since we are discussing the systems circle, this would be a good place to define *system* and *process*. The reader might ask why a book that assumes some working knowledge of TQM methodologies would find it necessary to do this. Two basic reasons exist: (1) The absence of clear descriptions in the quality literature

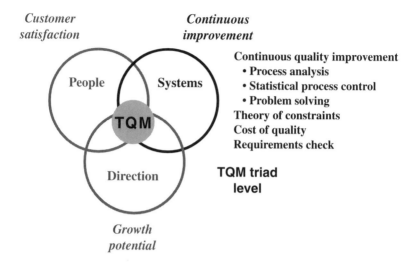

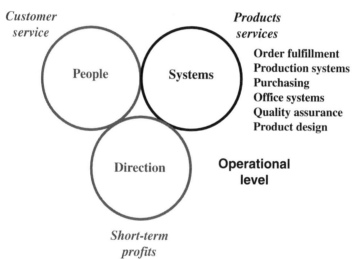

Figure 5.1: *The systems circles at the operational and TQM triad levels.*

and (2) the resultant vague use of the terms. Many books in the quality field jump right into the process/system terminology and, I guess, expect the reader to understand the meanings through the context. This results in multiple and conflicting meanings in the literature and in practice.

Is a System Just a Group of Processes?

Probably the most common confusion is using the word *system* to denote a group of processes. To test the extent of this perception I once asked a noted writer and lecturer in quality (in people-circle topics) what the difference was between a process and a system. The answer: "A system is a grouping of processes." So there it is—a herd of cattle, a gaggle of geese, and a system of processes. That usage really fouls up the understanding of concepts like "exact, documented system requirements must be established with operational definitions to support an error-free process." This leads to the most important third reason for addressing this issue here: The profound understanding of the interrelatedness of the quality tools and methodologies relies on distinct and precise definitions for process and system. These are two important pieces in the TQM puzzle.

These two words, which are adequately defined in any dictionary, are abused to the point of creating one more area of confusion for the new entrant to the TQM universe. The root cause of this blurring of the definitions may derive from the dictionary itself. If one reads far enough down the listing of definitions for each word, they tend to overlap and become similar to each other. Quality practitioners would be well-advised to stick to the first definition given for each word because there is a logical reason to require distinctly different definitions for process and system. The explanations and terminology of the quality tools, activities, and methodologies depend on the use of both words. We really must establish a level of precision in the use of words in our profession. Special contrary meanings for words, just serving the quality profession, generally serve no useful purpose. It's just more jargon for the confused novice.

The following are the first definitions listed for process and system from *Webster's Encyclopedic Unabridged Dictionary of the English Language.*

> *Process:* a systematic series of actions directed to some end.

System: an assemblage or combination of things or parts forming a complex or unitary whole.

Transforming these basic dictionary definitions by adding quality terminology without substantially changing the meanings produces these definitions.

Process: A series of activities that work on or with specified inputs to produce a desired output.

System: A group of interdependent elements or inputs, made up of material, procedures, equipment, facilities, and people, that together form a structure in which processes can operate.

Another way to distinguish between a system and a process is to look at how they can be documented. Flowcharts, one of the seven basic tools, are an effective tool for picturing, documenting, and understanding a process. A system, being more complicated than a process, is also more difficult to concisely document. System documentation will require a package of items that may include the following: (1) a layout drawing of the equipment location within the system; (2) a listing of the required staff to operate the processes in the system; (3) a list of the equipment in the system; (4) a list of the procedures needed to operate the processes; (5) a list of the supplies needed to support the operating processes; and (6) a complete list of requirements for the supplies, staff, procedures, equipment, and facilities.

The Interrelationship of Systems and Processes

Systems are static combinations of the just-mentioned inputs, while processes are dynamic uses of the systems through a planned series of action steps or tasks. Here are some examples of systems and processes.

System	Process
Hospital laboratory	Conducting a blood test
Computer	Preparing paychecks
Quality control department	Inspecting a sample of parts

Each of these systems support many individual processes. These processes could be interconnecting or separate. For example, the computer system contains the processes of preparing paychecks, constructing financial records, maintaining inventory records, and storing an address file database, to name a few. There are subparts to both systems and processes. One could define an entire organization as a system containing many smaller internal systems. A single, large, fairly complicated process would define an entire business, but, practically, we break it down into smaller processes for analysis and improvement activities.

Processes and systems are supported and defined by each other. Process revisions during problem-solving or continuous improvement activities may lead to a redesign of the system to support the revisions. For example, a decision to have a machine operator do SPC might include the need to add an SPC chart stand, measurement gages, and a calculator to the work area. Changing the process required a change in the system.

System revisions, many times caused by the availability of new technology, may require processes to be changed. A new machining fixture—a system change—eliminates some process steps that were previously needed to reposition a part for further machining. Changing to a paperless order entry system changes the ordering process. In both of these cases changing the system required a change in the process (Burns 1994).

Attributes of the Systems Circle— Placement Criteria

Continuous Improvement

This attribute is also the outcome resulting from actions taken in the systems circle. Certainly the most well-known methodology to produce continuous improvement is the CQI process, a process that is ongoing, as opposed to the single project–oriented reengineering methodology in the direction circle.

As indicated in chapter 1, the TQM triad does not differentiate—that is, use as placement criteria—the magnitude of the resultant improvements. Note that CQI stands for continuous quality improvement, not incremental quality improvement. A CQI team could complete a project with a 45 percent improvement, and a reengineering effort on a business process might only net a 12 percent gain. The true potential of CQI is grossly underestimated when it's labeled as incremental.

***Triad Theorem 13: Success or failure
is not measured in terms of percentage gain
on only one project, but on
long-term gains year after year.***

Team-Based, Directed, or Owned

The quality processes resident in this circle work well when controlled by teams, whether natural work teams or cross-functional teams. Most formal problem-solving processes are designed for and utilized by teams. Certainly, this does not preclude their utilization by an individual outside of the team environment.

Many opportunities for generating continuous improvement require ad hoc cross-functional teams. Projects such as eliminating damage complaints from airline baggage handling, reducing time spent waiting for an appointment at a medical clinic, or eliminating errors in home construction are all projects that would need team members from different departments or functional units.

Low Risk

An attribute of any quality program is the risk involved in not getting the planned outcome—or worse yet, the risk in causing damage to the organization's operating systems. Tools, activities, and methodologies implemented in the systems circle will practically always net increases in continuous improvement; therefore, low risk is considered an attribute related to Systems programs.

Certainly, the flagship program for this circle—CQI—exhibits the low-risk attribute. Why then, if it's low risk, does it seem so difficult to implement and keep in place? Many of the systems-circle quality programs, including CQI, do have high-risk strategic segments that are management's responsibility (direction circle). How to accomplish the required training, how to support teams, how to properly capture cost-of-quality savings, and how to create empowered employees are some of the questions that require strategic answers from management. Based on the understanding that a dichotomy does exist, if a program in the systems circle appears to be weak or failing, don't forget to check the direction circle strategies or the communications between the two circles.

Triad Theorem 14: A well-designed process in either the systems or people circle can fail without the support of the proper strategies from the direction circle.

Actually choosing an improvement project or an error elimination project and applying the CQI methodology will entail very little risk. A CQI team working through the steps of defining the project, identifying root causes, developing corrective action, and implementing corrective action has a very high probability of successfully producing measurable process improvement. Eliminating errors from or otherwise optimizing a process is a low-risk procedure—building on something that we know is already working, albeit working at a level we know can be improved. Reengineering, on the other hand, was considered high risk and placed in the direction circle, because one starts with a clean sheet of paper. There is no guarantee that the newly reengineered system will work better than or even as well as the one replaced.

Tools, Activities, and Methodologies

Here is a brief selection of tools, activities, and methodologies that are assigned to the systems circle. This coverage, along with the previously defined attributes, should give you the ability to place other quality programs in this list whether presently existing or newly emerging. Continuous quality improvement will be covered in detail because of its popularity and effectiveness. CQI also has the ability to show the interaction of many of the seven basic tools of quality with an improvement process.

Tools

There is a plethora of books available that provide excellent instructions and examples for the quality tools, so I won't reinvent the wheel in this book. The objectives here will be to strengthen the unified total quality model by examining how the tools are combined with the methodologies and to address certain flaws that can weaken the model.

The Seven Basic Tools of Quality. This is the accepted home of the seven basic tools, although I have previously indicated their importance in all three of the triad circles at both levels. These tools are one more piece in the TQM puzzle and, as such, develop their full potential when linked with various methodologies—for instance, CQI, benchmarking, and reengineering. An example of this linking is found in the following Methodologies section when the three-step CQI process is discussed. Two of the tools have especially been abused by having this linking synergism ignored and being used instead as standalone elements.

Department heads become absorbed in having their staff flowchart all the department's processes ostensibly to provide documentation of their procedures. It ends up being an exercise in filling notebooks with complicated flowcharts that are only looked at when an auditor passes through. There is a wealth of improvement opportunities pictured in these volumes of flowcharts that never gets addressed. If the department head would use the flowcharts to fuel departmental continuous improvement, the staff might become motivated to do more of this quality "stuff."

The other tool that tends to become what someone before me labeled "expensive corporate wallpaper" is the control chart. The charts are usually put on the walls to once again prove something to visiting auditors, and the vast mother lode of information is never mined. I'm reminded of the cartoon where the manager is pointing out a special chart on a wall full of charts, saying, "This is my chart that shows how many charts we are doing." Once again, if a process was in place to take advantage of the information the control charts display, staff members might change their opinion of charting being a waste of time.

Triad Theorem 15: A chart may be worth a thousand words, but action is worth a thousand charts.

By the way, do you think it went unnoticed by upper management that large amounts of resources, both staff time and training budget, went into developing proficiency in the use of these tools with no apparent payoff on the bottom line?

My experience indicates that few teams ever develop competency with the seven basic tools—competency being defined as the capability to use effectively all seven tools, to understand the information given by the tools, and to know when in the problem-solving process to use them. Different road blocks impede the development of the competency. Lack of suitable training and facilitation leaves the team unfamiliar with the tools or unsure as to when they should be applied. Another major road block is the "statistics anxiety" that may develop when math and statistics are introduced in the training. The first perception by many team members is that this is too difficult— there must be an easier way—so competency never has a chance to develop.

The lack of suitable training is an issue that is many times connected with the problem of statistics anxiety. The training is so complicated and lengthy that only the engineers in the class make it through with their minds still functioning. Training will be covered in chapter 8; for now the important outcome should be team members that are capable of understanding the two types of variation, can read the various charts, and know how important data are to generating continuous improvement.

The team facilitator plays a key role. When the team members come out of the seven basic tools training with the just-listed capabilities, the facilitator's job is to assist them in developing the previously defined competency. When a team has been led through the problem-solving process and is rewarded with a successful outcome, the use of the tools is reinforced. Demonstrated real-world benefits are the only way to sell employees and management on the usefulness and power of the seven basic tools of quality.

Cost of Quality. It's interesting to note how tools that have been misused to the point of discarding them in frustration can become strong, viable elements of a TQM system. They transform from short-lived fads to powerful tools when coupled with other tools, activities, and methodologies, using the understanding gained from the TQM triad. Some tools won't effectively help an organization's quality effort if operating alone, but gain their effectiveness when installed in a system. This tool, the cost of quality, may be the best example of this phenomenon.

Utilizing cost accounting techniques outside the realm of traditional accounting procedures to more accurately gauge an organization's operation and quality processes has been discussed since the early 1950s. Two of the important early contributors to this concept were J. M. Juran and A. V. Feigenbaum. The ASQC Quality Costs Committee first assembled the information in a booklet titled *Quality Costs—What & How* in 1967, followed by *Principles of Quality Costs,* published in 1990. The idea of product and service nonconformances having costs that are many times hidden, that if eliminated will more than pay for the costs of elimination and usually net important profits, was popularized in Philip Crosby's book *Quality Is Free.* Crosby (1984, 85) further promoted a cost of quality (COQ) concept as the fourth of his four absolutes of quality: "The measurement of quality is the price of nonconformance."

Quality experts' emphasis of this tool seemed to turn into an overemphasis by many organizations practicing quality improvement. Stories abound about companies investing massive amounts of resources to collect, tabulate, and chart COQ data on their entire operation. The effort was meant to facilitate the formation of teams to eliminate the failure costs of quality and to measure improvements due to the companywide quality process. After attempting the data collection for a period of time, the discovery is usually made that, as a companywide management tool, COQ is a failure. Not enough detail exists to identify quality improvement projects, and the inherent inaccuracies in the collection process many times obliterate improvement trends that may be present. This is not proof of the failure of COQ as a tool, however. It proves the point made in chapter 3: The failure is that of placing the tool in the direction circle. It is a failure of implementation.

Numerous examples are presented in this book illustrating the use of COQ in the systems circle and as the communication link between Systems and Direction. The TQM triad demonstrates the value and the necessity of using this tool that previously was in danger of being eliminated from organizations' TQM systems because of misuse and misunderstanding.

A definition and short description of the COQ tool follow, to assist the reader unfamiliar with the tool in the understanding of upcoming COQ examples.

> *Cost of quality:* A method of documenting (1) the costs involved in preventing or inspecting for failures in an organization's products and services and (2) the costs caused by failures of an organization's products and services, both before and after delivery.

This tool clearly conveys the effect of poor quality on the bottom line of the profit statement. Therefore, it can provide the driving force for management to initiate the installation of quality improvement processes. COQ puts the potential and success measure of the continuous improvement processes in the systems circle in terms familiar to upper management—dollars.

Each of the two classifications noted in the definition are further divided into two separate but related categories. Each cost category contains many elements, some of which are unique to certain types of businesses. "Quality cost *elements* are the detailed functions, tasks, or expenses which, when properly combined, make up the quality cost *categories*" (Campanella 1990, 23). Following is a list of example quality cost elements for each category.

Category 1. Prevention: Costs of developing, implementing, and supporting the organization's quality system.

Prevention cost elements include the following:
a. CQI team meetings
b. Quality training
c. Quality administrative salaries
d. Quality systems audits
e. Quality manual development
f. Customer surveys

Category 2. Appraisal: Costs of maintaining quality levels by means of product and service evaluations.

Appraisal cost elements include the following:
a. Incoming inspection of purchased material
b. Expensed cost of inspection equipment
c. Inspection and tests of products
d. Reviewing inspection data
e. Checking for errors on process paperwork

Category 3. Internal failure: Costs incurred when products and services are discovered to not meet the customers' requirements before shipment.

Internal failure cost elements include the following:
a. Review of defective products
b. Handling and storage of defective products
c. Redoing an earlier operation
d. Reinspecting the redo or rework
e. Scrapped product
f. Tracking down missing information on paperwork

Category 4. External failure: Costs incurred when products and services do not meet the customers' requirements after receipt by the customer.

External failure cost elements include the following:

a. Time required to receive and record complaints
b. Repairing or replacing returned product
c. Recall activities
d. Warranty claims
e. Redoing a service activity
f. Delivering a missing item from the original service
g. Discounts offered to satisfy a complaint

CQI teams are usually focusing on the failure costs of quality, categories 3 and 4. Compiling a dollar amount representing the total of the elements that are contributing to the team's assigned project is one of the first team actions. This is an effective measure of the CQI project's cost savings potential and, as such, will need to be communicated to management.

Activities

These are actions by individuals or teams that support the continuous improvement methodologies and the systems-circle processes. Two representative activities in Systems are (1) the requirements check on process inputs and outputs and (2) the development of operational definitions.

Requirements Check. If our quality definition for this circle is to meet customers' requirements, then we must have an effective method of gathering all the requirements and documenting them for future use. All the requirements include those for the process inputs as well as the outputs. The process of defining or establishing requirements is a two-way communication between customer and supplier. The supplier starts this discussion by questioning and listening to the customer, and together they transform needs and expectations into customer requirements. Forms can be developed that list all the outputs, inputs, customers, and suppliers to facilitate the recording of the requirements. The process operator, forms in hand, can seek out the various suppliers and customers on the requirements check form and develop the requirements in a customer–supplier discussion.

This important concept is usually a part of most organizations' TQM systems, at least for external customers and suppliers. Just as important is the need to apply the same rigorous technique within and between the circles at the operational level.

Requirements check within a circle. Operational-level processes in the systems circle must interface based on a thorough understanding of the requirements.

One of the internal suppliers for the blood donation room of the County Blood Center is the staff responsible for scheduling blood donors. The schedulers know that the phlebotomists can manage six donors per hour, so they have been scheduling six to arrive each hour on the hour. This grouping of the donors is causing difficulty with both the donor history interview process and the blood collecting process. The donation room CQI team is going to meet with the scheduling department to work out better scheduling requirements as a step toward reducing the average donor time at the center (Burns 1994).

Requirements check between circles. The people and direction circles interact to acquire and retain customers by developing (Direction) and implementing (People) innovative customer service processes. In other words, strategy is set by management and carried out by the staff. This interaction must be based on a solid foundation of agreed-upon requirements.

A well-known hotel chain has empowered its front-desk employees to personally make decisions about how to handle customer complaints. The employees have been given a $200 limit per complaint occurrence on the cost of the decisions they make. It's expected that the resultant quick response to dissatisfied customers will greatly improve customer satisfaction; no more "I'll need to ask the manager about that." If the $200 limit is the only requirement communicated from management, this customer complaint service process will likely fail from lack of requirements. The failure would come as a dissatisfaction by managers over the types of decisions being made. Management must develop a framework of requirements that will give the front-desk employee the ability to make responsible decisions that reflect management's customer service philosophy and the mission of the hotel chain.

Requirements check between the triad and operational levels. This is the third type of internal interaction needing a requirements check.

We return to the hotel front desk to find an example. Management is very pleased with the decisions being made by front-desk employees as they use their discretion, based on the framework of requirements, to handle customer complaints; however, management is not pleased with the cost of this customer service program. It's not the fault of abusing the $200 limit; it's just that there are too many complaints. A cross-functional CQI team is being formed to eliminate customer complaints. One of the first actions the team took was to develop a reporting form for customer complaints. The team needed to know what types of problems existed and which were the most frequent. The team worked with the front-desk employees to establish requirements for recording complaints, knowing that complete and firm requirements would go a long way toward ensuring accurate data.

Operational Definitions. (Operational definitions were defined in chapter 2, and the term *quality profits* was given an operational definition in chapter 4.) Many of the process measurements taken in the course of continuous quality improvement may be subjective. This subjectivity can cause variation in the measurement process between people taking the same measurements or from day to day with the same person. An operational definition will provide a systematic procedure for acquiring meaningful data. Every quality measure needs an operational definition for counting, gauging, or visually inspecting the attribute of a product or service being studied. Operational definitions can also be used anywhere that ambiguity will cause difficulty in interactions throughout the unified total quality model, whether it's in defining quality or explaining requirements.

Operational definitions and CQI team measurements. There will be many occasions where CQI teams must turn over the task of collecting necessary data to process operators. The process operators, being the process experts, are in a good position to count process errors, measure cycle times, or list types of complaints. CQI project analysis—and therefore project solutions—rely on the accuracy of collected information about nonconformances or performance. If the data input to a CQI project is perceived to be inaccurate, team members will lose interest in striving for meaningful solutions or the project outcome will be questioned by outsiders aware of the data inconsistencies. Our high-tech computer friends have a saying for this, "Garbage in—garbage out."

The Valley Clinic was concerned about the waiting time spent by patients before starting into the actual process of seeing the health care providers. The clinic CQI team members weren't sure they could solve the problem, but the team knew the first item of business was learning about the problem. So far, all they knew was that 10 percent to 15 percent of the patients complained. The decision was made by the team to collect data on wait times for a one-month period. They proceeded to construct an operational definition for the measurements they wanted. This would be used as a training aid and reference for the actual data collectors.

Here is an operational definition for Valley Clinic patient wait times.

1. *Define the characteristic to be measured.* The patient wait time from when the patient checks in at the receptionist's desk to the time when a nurse or assistant escorts them to a room.
2. *Choose a measurement device.* The clock on the waiting room wall will be used. It is not to be reset while patients are waiting.

3. *Describe the method for measurement.* Every patient will be given a 3″ × 5″ time card by the receptionist at check-in. The receptionist will enter the present time, date, and initials of the first health care provider to be seen. When the nurse calls a patient to be escorted to a patient room, the card will be collected and the present time entered. All times will be to the nearest minute. If a special circumstance develops that would affect the wait time, write it in the *notes* section on the card.

4. *State the decision criteria for evaluation of the resulting measurements.* No accept/reject decision is required. All the cards will be collected by the CQI team for analysis.

Imagine the measurement variability in the data if all the data collectors had used their own watches or if different start and stop points had been used by various collectors. This definition ensures uniformity in the data collection process, a solid start for the CQI team. Operational definitions become an important communication tool between the systems circle at the TQM triad level and the systems circle at the operational level. This clear and precise definition documents and communicates the requirements determined in the requirements check for a customer–supplier transaction between these two circles.

Operational definitions and requirements. After a requirements check has been finished, there may be a need to construct operational definitions for a few of the requirements. If two people could interpret a requirement differently, it is ambiguous and must be operationally defined to prevent any misunderstanding. The following are some sample requirements.

Requirement 1: The form must be typed. This is not ambiguous—no need for an operational definition.

Requirement 2: Ship in the provided carton by UPS standard ground shipment in quantities of 144. Again, this is very clear—no further definition is required.

Requirement 3: A hotel housekeeping requirement: The carpet must be cleaned after each guest use of the room. Definitely ambiguous, needs an operational definition, as would *the beds must be properly made.*

Operational definitions paired with a requirements check become a powerful operational-level communication device. The result is clearly defined requirements between linked processes (Systems), between processes and external customers (People), or between processes and management (Direction).

Methodologies

These are the powerhouse systems of methods, principles, and rules that provide the framework for using the tools and activities to reach an expected outcome. They, therefore, contribute a large part of the continuous improvement outcome for the systems circle. Two of the constituents of this category that are similar and interrelated are CQI and theory of constraints (TOC).

Continuous Quality Improvement. CQI has already been defined, and there are many examples in this book of its use within the context of the TQM triad. Since this book assumes your basic understanding of quality improvement, the focus here will be on the interrelationship of CQI and the seven basic tools.

The unified total quality model does just what the name implies: It unifies the constituents of the TQM system. The CQI process takes this unification to the next level. It becomes a model that unifies the quality tools. Within CQI there is, in addition to the unification, an inherent order to the application of the tools (see Figure 5.2).

Figure 5.2 shows the dynamics involved in solving a process problem using the seven basic tools. Most improvement projects, whether conducted by individuals or teams, need to pass through the three steps: standardize, stabilize, and problem elimination. Skipping one or both of the first two steps can result in inadequate or flawed solutions to the problem. Benefits

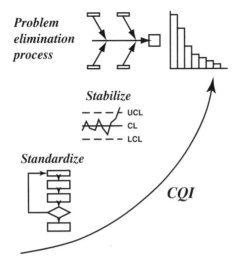

Figure 5.2: *The continuous quality improvement process.*

are derived from each step; thus, the organization will see payoffs after each is completed.

1. *Standardize.* Why must the process flowchart and standardizing come first? A primary root cause of process problems may be the absence of a standard operating procedure that every process operator diligently follows. Three reasons exist for this situation.
   a. Certainly the most basic reason is that no one ever took the time to design the process in question. Process operators were expected to do their jobs with a little training and a lot of common sense.
   b. No emphasis was placed on the importance of following the standard operating procedure as documented. It's in the notebook for the system auditor to see.
   c. Process evolution occurred; each operator adjusted the process to his or her personal satisfaction. Being innovative and redesigning the process is great; but it should be done in a structured approach, with everyone involved in the process going the same direction.

No process analysis can be accomplished, whether it's measurement or problem solving, if no common process exists or an existing one is not followed. The most predictable comment heard in a meeting when team members are attempting to flowchart their process is, "Oh, is that how you do it?"

A process flowchart becomes another communication device within the process, between processes, and between management and the process. When the process has been flowcharted and we are certain that every process operator is following the same procedure, the next CQI step can be taken.

Just accomplishing step 1 will net gains in process quality improvement. In fact, there are isolated instances where this is all that's needed. Just getting "everyone on the same page" can produce surprising results. Team members should not be concerned if their process as presently operated and flowcharted looks inefficient, has non–value-added steps, or contains redo loops. The objective of this step is standardization. Step 3 will offer the opportunity to redesign the present process.

2. *Stabilize.* This is the step that's usually skipped—it's "too hard." Not only is a baseline measurement important to measure process improvements against, but before going on to the third step, we need to be assured that the process is stable. Stabilizing the process means

   a. Using control charts to display key quality data from the process—for example, errors, cycle time, a critical dimension, or complaint calls.
   b. Identifying the presence of signals of process instability. If a signal is seen in the chart, there is a good chance a special cause is affecting the process.
   c. Look for the root cause (usually a singular one) that represents the special cause. This will be the first problem-solving activity for the team.
   d. Take corrective action against the root cause to ensure its permanent elimination.
   e. Check for a stable process by continuing to monitor the control chart.

The removal of one or more special causes will produce the second level of measurable quality improvement. Stabilizing the process may not change the average on the chart for the number of errors, cycle time, or whatever else was being measured. But the excessive variability induced by special causes has been eliminated, which will result in a consistent and predictable process.

Skipping this step wreaks havoc with the team's efforts to generate continuous improvement. Without some assurance of a stable process to analyze, the team can only expect a process with no predictability. It's very much like trying to shoot at a randomly moving target.

As with the flowchart, the control chart is a communication devise between the systems and direction circles. Controllers of the CQI process residing in the direction circle, often called the steering committee, use the control chart to monitor team progress and results.

3. *Problem elimination process.* After the CQI team is certain of uniformity and stability of the process, the real problem solving begins. The team can follow the problem-solving methodology selected by the organization. There are many excellent ones available, all following the same basic steps and utilizing the seven basic tools.

This overview of the three-step CQI process demonstrates the important links between the seven basic tools, the CQI methodology, and the direction circle. Being aware of these links and keeping them functioning enhances the operation of the systems circle.

Theory of Constraints. As with CQI, the need for underlying philosophies to be internalized by management (Direction) before implementation is attempted cannot be overemphasized. This methodology specifically has a very strong management element. In fact, it's so strong that I contemplated putting this in the direction circle. Readers who have used theory of constraints in their organizations may wish to move it to management's circle if their experiences indicate that this placement is more representative of its application.

> *Theory of constraints:* An ongoing improvement process of identifying and eliminating system constraints (bottlenecks) to increase throughput.

This methodology gained prominence with the popularity of *The Goal* by Eliyahu M. Goldratt and Jeff Cox. In Goldratt's (1990) later book on the subject, *Theory of Constraints,* he pokes fun at the term *profound knowledge;* however, his books are arguably the best place to gain insight into the fourth of Deming's (1993) four-part system of profound knowledge—psychology. In fact, a chapter in *Theory of Constraints* is "The Devastating Impact of the Organization's Psychology."

TOC has a lot in common with CQI, and they also have a synergistic relationship. Goldratt (1990, ix) emphasizes that "improvement, no matter how big, is not sufficient. Only a process of ongoing improvement can sustain a company's excellent performance in the long run." Ongoing improvement certainly is a philosophy compatible with CQI and the systems circle. He goes on to say that of the three ways to gain performance improvement (increase throughput, decrease inventory, or decrease operating expense), increasing throughput offers the highest potential for improvement (1990, 91). His theory is based on the understanding that bottlenecks control throughput and, therefore, must be continuously improved to increase process throughput.

If we want to look at what most differentiates the methodologies of CQI and TOC, it would be that CQI is a more general approach while TOC focuses on increasing throughput. The synergism relationship can be seen if TOC is positioned as one of the sources for CQI projects. When a bottleneck (constraint) is located in an organization, the elimination may require the formation of a CQI team to develop corrective action. In fact, if there is a choice between an improvement project involving a system constraint and one elsewhere in the system, the constraint should be dealt with first. Improving nonbottlenecks will not increase throughput; eliminating the constraints will.

Since TOC involves dealing with accounting systems, material flow through the system, staffing of systems, utilization of equipment, and many other organization-wide processes and systems, it's imperative that management take a leading role here. Teams working on TOC-driven projects would need to be made up of management and staff—management to deal with the big organization-wide issues, and staff to provide the expertise on the constraints. So in the final analysis, TOC is a shared methodology with the direction circle.

These systems-circle tools, activities, and methodologies include many communicators. These communicators are action steps that cause necessary information to be conveyed and result in good business decisions being made. They represent important links between the circles, within the circles, and between the levels. Each communicator added by an organization strengthens its TQM system.

Interaction of the TQM Triad and Operational Levels

Figure 5.3 traces the path of many of the interactions discussed in this chapter. TQM quickly loses its luster for management if it can't demonstrate measurable results in the real world. This figure illustrates how the TQM system interacts with the operational-level processes to produce those results. To simplify Figure 5.3, methodology will be assumed to also include the tools and activities that reside in the systems circle.

The whole process of generating the continuous improvement outcome starts at the top of the figure with the selection of a continuous improvement methodology that will cause improved output of operational-level processes. This improved output can be measured by the level of conformance of the product or service to customers' requirements. We are reminded

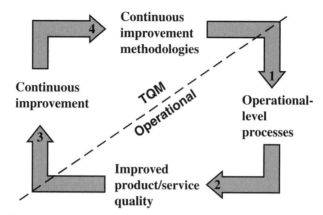

Figure 5.3: *The continuous improvement interaction cycle.*

that requirements include much more than specifications. Also included are quantity, consistency, on-time delivery, cost, product safety, and performance, just to name a few. Therefore, continuous improvement methodologies that seem to affect the process more than the output really do have a major impact on product and service quality.

A CQI project that cuts 15 percent off the process cycle time may not change the defect level in the product or service, but it certainly will affect the cost and on-time delivery of the product or service. The point here is that any activity that improves the process will affect the output quality, as defined by its operational definition.

Successes and Failures of the Interaction Cycle

Failures of continuous improvement methodologies occur when the process of Figure 5.3 does not go full cycle. Usually the break is at step 2. For example, management decrees that everyone in the manufacturing plant will use SPC. (We hear from the direction circle!) SPC, a continuous improvement tool, is then force applied to all the machining processes. Management walks through the plant and is pleased. Auditors view the high level of participation and are satisfied. What is easily hidden from view, either purposely or unknowingly, is the embarrassing fact that no processes, products, or services show improved quality.

In fact, interviewing the machine operators would probably cause one to believe the processes were actually slowed by the added work of charting.

If the success of the continuous improvement effort is gauged by the number of CQI teams, number of process operators using SPC, or number of process flowcharts drawn, the measurement is focusing only on step 1. This can happen when the motivation for implementing continuous improvement is to satisfy a customer's requirement so as to remain a certified vendor or to satisfy a third party's requirements for having a quality plan in place. The resultant focus is on making sure the organization is doing the right things and not on demonstrating continuous quality improvement. Organizations caught up in this game become quite skillful in putting on "quality dog-and-pony shows" for the auditors, but behind the scenes there is no substance. A strange phenomenon sometimes develops where top management starts to believe its own hype. Sooner or later managers realize that the effort expended is not producing positive or measurable results, and it's on to the next quality buzzword fad.

Continuous improvement facilitators not only make sure teams accomplish their project tasks, but also assist process managers in facilitating step 2. The true success of step 1, applying a continuous improvement methodology to an operational-level process, is measured by the actual improvement that occurs in step 2. Just as step 1 takes a strong commitment in training and implementation, step 2 will require a strong commitment by management to produce real results from the as-yet-potential results. The use of cost of quality to drive the improvement in step 2 for CQI projects is discussed in chapters 7 and 8.

The manufacturing plant with the SPC implementation problem is a different case. Often, the diligent practice of SPC is, in fact, improving product quality. The process is knocking at the door of step 2, but no one seems to notice or take the correct follow-up action. One manufacturer took the bold step of removing in-process inspection by the quality control department from parts that were machined with the critical dimensions being monitored by a control chart. That did cause people to notice. Machined parts inspection had become a redundant step, but the cost savings weren't realized until management took the proper step.

Once past the oft-forgotten step 2, it's all downhill. Each effective application of a continuous improvement methodology to an operational-level process produces a positive change in process output quality. Improved product and service quality from each circuit around the interaction cycle additively generates the continuous improvement outcome. Positive outcomes become the driving force for continuation of a cycle that is producing profitable results for the organization. And the cycle continues.

Measure of Success

Measuring the success of quality improvement processes in the systems circle follows a parallel procedure as that for Direction. In chapter 4, before measuring the improved quality of short-term profits, the term *quality profits* had to be operationally defined. One way to determine success in Systems at the TQM triad level is by measuring the improved quality of the outputs (products and services) at the operational level. An operational definition for quality products and services is needed and will be derived from the Systems quality definition (see chapter 2): meeting the customers' requirements. Certainly another measure of success for this circle would be the increased operational performance of the processes and systems. An operational definition could be written for performance measures of productivity, rework reduction, or cycle time.

An operational definition for quality products and services follows.

1. *Define the characteristic to be measured.* The level of conformance to customers' requirements.
2. *Choose a measurement device.* The requirements check form for process output that documents customer requirements for all aspects of the product or service,

including but not limited to specifications, quantity, safety, packaging, delivery, cost, and service after the sale.
3. *Describe the method for measurement.* Compare the product or service to the documented requirements.
4. *State the decision criteria for evaluation of the resulting measurements.* The product or service is considered a quality unit if all the requirements are met.

An increase in the number of units meeting the decision criteria the first time checked can be a valid measure of the success of continuous improvement activities. There is an underlying difficulty, though, in just taking the measurement to this level of detail. It does indicate the improved quality of the product or service, but it tends to hide potential cost savings that need to be communicated to the direction circle. The success at generating continuous improvement, project by project, may be measured in minutes saved per production cycle, errors eliminated per 100 client forms, or percentage reduction in scrapped parts. The common denominator is dollars—all projects are measured in terms of the cost of quality, the measure of the effectiveness of cost reduction methodologies.

An insurance company claims department decided to form a CQI team to focus on the elimination of errors from claim forms received from its claims adjustors. Through innovative changes in the form, switching to online computer submittal, and some procedures training, the problem was completely eliminated. Did this save the insurance company any money? Not yet. If the measure is limited to showing a decrease from 17 errors per 100 forms to zero, the true potential cost savings is hidden. Management notes the results in monthly reports, the workers are thanked, and everyone goes back to business as usual. Using the cost of quality to measure the improved quality will indicate what actions will result in actual capture of the cost savings and, in turn, a payoff for investing time in CQI team activities.

In our insurance example, one of the COQ elements was the cost involved in tracking down the correct information—labor and telephone calls. One employee spent an average of two hours per day on this task. The insurance company will truly save money when that two hours is applied to value-added work that was previously done by temporary help or when 10 hours per week is eliminated from labor expense.

A cost-of-quality report from a CQI team project may then become the preferred measure of improved product, service, and process quality. An operational definition constructed around this measure of success would describe the measurement method and resulting report format. A monthly or quarterly summary of potential cost-of-quality savings and/or captured cost-of-quality savings documents the continuous improvement outcome for the covered reporting time period.

 **Chapter 6**

The People Circle

Introduction

We finish our tour around the TQM triad with an examination of the people circle, the home of the process experts and the complement to the systems circle (see Figure 6.1). This part of the triad represents the "soft" side of total quality, whereas the methodologies in the systems circle are often labeled the "hard" side. The people in this component of the model deal with customers, often in one-on-one interactions. Customers important to the organization are in different constituencies: the external customers (bill-paying customers), the internal customers (staff in downstream processes), and team customers (fellow members of teams). The last could be considered a subset of internal customers, but worthwhile to treat separately for some of the techniques used in this interaction—for example, reaching a consensus and effectively participating in self-directed work teams.

Customer Service Starts at Home

Total quality customer satisfaction thrives in an environment where the three customer types are understood and managed as separate units. An organization building this environment believes that employees' attitudes while servicing external customers reflect the quality of customer service they receive as

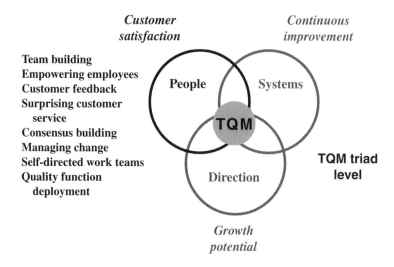

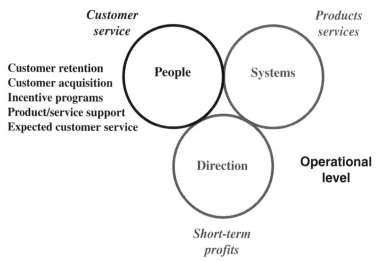

Figure 6.1: *The people circles at the operational and TQM triad levels.*

internal customers. Internal treatment of people is the foundation for causing external customer satisfaction. In other words, the paying customer comes second behind the organization's own employees.

***Triad Theorem 16: Employees' attitudes
while servicing external customers reflect the***

> *quality of customer service they receive*
> *as internal customers.*

A Taco with Your Name on It

Examples abound attesting to the success of the philosophy of the employee first from individual retail businesses to large chain operations. A fast-food restaurant in Marshalltown, Iowa (population approximately 25,000), has received recognition for being the sales leader for its franchise the past seven years.

Employees are treated well. They are given regular raises, have access to partial tuition assistance at the local community college, and have major holidays off.

Managers are treated well. They receive bonuses, profit sharing, and two days off each week. They work approximately 40 hours per week while other fast-food restaurant managers may work 60 to 70 hours per week.

These benefits are practically unheard of in fast-food retailing, and the resultant job satisfaction is reflected in an employee turnover rate one would expect to find in a manufacturing company. For instance, the two managers have been with the business for 12 years and 17 years. This low turnover is instrumental in creating a high level of customer service. When you become a regular customer—and you will after experiencing the quality of the total experience—the staff greet you by name when you come in to place your order. How do they learn your name? They have a standard system of calling you back to the counter when your order is ready, but they don't use numbers—they use first names. The process of long-time employees asking customers for their name when taking their order creates an environment conducive to learning customers' names and remembering them.

One secret to the business owner's success, then, is her balancing the people and systems circles. Processes have been designed to serve the employee as well as the customer. These employee-friendly processes help create the environment in the people circle to support the generation of customer satisfaction.

The Motto Tells the Story

A 1992 Malcolm Baldrige National Quality Award winner has the employee-first philosophy right in their motto: "We are Ladies and Gentlemen Serving Ladies and Gentlemen." Note who comes first in the Ritz-Carlton employee motto. Each employee receives more than 100 hours of quality training, has many opportunities for recognition, and is empowered to "move heaven and earth to satisfy a customer" (Ritz-Carlton 1993).

As with the fast-food restaurant, the Ritz-Carlton also balances the people and systems circles. Each employee understands the quality tools, and they're involved in both standing problem-solving teams and special quality improvement teams. Their employee selection process, training, and quality improvement efforts have paid off with a companywide staff turnover rate less than half the industry average.

Attributes of the People Circle — Placement Criteria

People Oriented — Individual Interaction Focused

Techniques and activities with this attribute are practiced at the individual level in a customer–supplier interaction. The focus here is personal skills that enhance this interaction, whether it be with a paying customer, downstream process, or CQI team member. If we label every communication between two or more individuals a customer–supplier interaction, then techniques and activities that enhance communication-type personal skills are extremely important to the people circle and the TQM system.

Many of the techniques and activities that meet this criterion are specifically for strengthening individual relationships within teams with secondary benefits for the more traditional customer–supplier relationships.

Customer Oriented — Customer Satisfaction Focused

This attribute is also the outcome resulting from action taken in this circle. Certainly, just about any activity in the TQM system is in some way connected to customer satisfaction. It is not at all unusual for a CQI project in the systems circle to generate customer satisfaction as a secondary outcome. This is represented by the overlap of the TQM triad circles.

The CQI team for an airline was able to reduce the time to move baggage between connecting flights. This project was started to help get the airplanes away from the gate more quickly to make room for incoming flights (on-time departures was not the problem). In the new process fewer bags were lost, which certainly helped the customer satisfaction ratings.

What will be placed here are the techniques and activities that directly focus on providing customer service and generating customer satisfaction. This includes the aggregate actions taken to affect quality products and services in a way that surprises and delights the customer, or the surprising actions taken to rectify a product or service problem. Techniques are also included that gauge the customers' perception and acceptance of the present level of customer service—for instance, customer satisfaction surveys.

Process Oriented—Group Interaction Focused

Techniques and activities that exhibit this attribute are usually related to strengthening the team approach used in the systems circle. These teams could be self-directed work teams at the operational level or ad hoc cross-functional teams at the TQM triad level. Both types require similar techniques to function, although their objectives are different. Also included here would be the new techniques required by supervisors and managers to enable them to shift to coaching roles in the TQM system.

Techniques and Activities

This circle could probably be characterized as the one with no dominant methodologies; instead there is a spectrum of techniques and activities available. They can be classified by their predominant attribute: people oriented, customer oriented, or process oriented. There seems to be a plethora of training available; trainers, consultants, and community colleges are prepared to assist with this soft side of quality. The following list is a selection of the course subjects or titles in each of the three attribute areas.

People Oriented
Conflict resolution
Listening/communication skills
Employee recognition
Consensus building
Dealing with change
Confrontation skills
Peer appraisal and feedback
Skill-based pay systems

Customer Oriented
Creating surprising service
Getting customer feedback
Designing customer surveys
Evaluating survey data
Building customer relationships
Creating customer-focused teams
Building customer loyalty

Process Oriented
Supervisors as coaches
Team building
Creating self-directed work teams
Empowering employees
Facilitating teams
Managing group dynamics

Interaction of the TQM Triad and Operational Levels

Two Levels of Customer Service

Generating an increased level of customer satisfaction follows the same process of interactions as in the other two circles; however, there are two distinct levels of customer service, correlating with the TQM triad and operational levels, that combine to form the customers' total experience with the product or service. In other words, the customer service supplier must be aware of and manage two levels, but the customer only perceives customer service as a single entity.

We Expect a Certain Level of Customer Service. At the operational level, customer service is offered as part of the product or service package. This will be labeled *expected* customer service. With the purchase of computer software we expect customer support telephone access to extricate us from the endless array of pull-down menus. When we purchase a small appliance from the local Huge-Mart, we expect to be able to return it if it fails to perform to our expectations. If we have a complaint concerning a restaurant meal, we expect to have it corrected. When we check in at a hotel, we expect assistance in getting our luggage to the room.

Employees can be trained to provide the level of expected customer service their employer has deemed necessary to satisfy their customers. Expected customer service requirements, processes, and operational definitions can be established the same way they were for the product or service. Like product and service expectations, businesses must be always aware of changing customer service expectations in the marketplace.

Surprise Me with Customer Service. Customer service influenced by the TQM triad builds on the expected customer service foundation with hundreds of added refinements provided by empowered employees. They hope to delight us—if they do, we are usually surprised; hence *surprising* customer service. Since these customer service improvements are unexpected, the examples tend to be unique for each occurrence. Each empowered employee is introducing his or her own distinctive brand of excellence to the customer service package to cause increased customer satisfaction.

After many experiences of a certain surprising customer service, it can become part of the customers' expectations and will need to be added to the expected customer service package.

Note that for an organization to provide surprising customer service requires a level of employee empowerment. An employee can be trained to provide the expected customer service package consistently and correctly; however, only guidelines and parameters can be provided in training employees to provide surprising service. Two employees in the same position in the same business could arrive at different surprising-service actions when confronted with the same customer experience. Here, exactness is not possible or even desired, and correctness only has a meaning within the context of the organization's guidelines and parameters for surprising service. This context was labeled the framework of requirements (see chapter 5) that allows employees to make decisions that are consistent and compatible with what management would do in the same situation.

These surprises come in two categories: (1) embellishments to the expected level during normal customer service, and (2) extraordinary actions taken by empowered employees following failure of an organization's product or service or during times of crisis. The first is a pleasant surprise on top of a good customer service experience. Examples of this are having your name used by an employee of the servicing company when you wouldn't expect it; receiving a call from the hotel's restaurant shortly after checking in, asking if you'd like a complimentary beverage delivered to your room; and having the auto service shop wash your car when you take it in for an oil change.

The second is a surprise that is attempting to smooth over a bad customer service experience, whether it is the fault of the servicing organization or not. Examples here might be having the manager of a hotel find you a room at a competitor's hotel *and* personally drive you there after the first hotel accidently overbooked; ordering a dessert offered by the waiter only to be told later that the restaurant is out and receiving a free coupon for next time; or having your bank take extraordinary measures to salvage your vacation when you have your cash and credit cards stolen.

A bank in West Des Moines, Iowa, had automated transaction machines at two of its drive-up lanes go out of service. Two tellers volunteered to become carhops on in-line skates to service the long lines of customers. A systems breakdown that could have generated a lot of irate customers was turned into an experience the customers actually enjoyed. One of the tellers reported many customers teasing her about taking orders for cheeseburgers and fries (Elbert 1996).

The Customer Satisfaction Interaction Cycle

The 4-Star Hotel management team decided as part of its new customer satisfaction strategy that front-desk staff would be empowered to make more decisions regarding customer service. The first step, of course, was a thorough staff training in the expected customer service requirements and the surprising customer service guidelines. Managers were firm in their conviction that the expected customer service had to be met each and every time—zero defects. If there was a failure at this level, they wanted the staff to be able to immediately resolve the situation. The customer satisfaction interaction cycle can only be effective in this environment.

Step 1 (see Figure 6.2). The combined activities of empowering front-desk employees and providing guidelines for surprising service are applied to the processes of assisting guests at check-in and checkout. The team of front-desk employees has been meeting every Monday to share stories of surprising service the team members personally offered in the past week.

Step 2. This constant attention to the extras affects the level of the hotel's customer service quality in the team's area of responsibility. The measurement of this is fed back to the team as results from surveys conducted based on the operational definition for customer service quality (see the next section).

Step 3. Survey results with a positive trend indicate that the actions are working. The increasing quality of the 4-Star Hotel's front-desk customer service, including both the expected and surprising elements, is generating higher customer satisfaction. This leads to step 4.

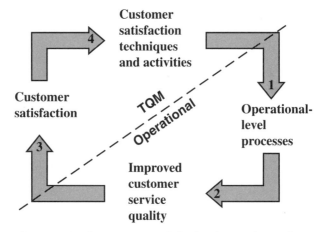

Figure 6.2: *The customer satisfaction interaction cycle.*

Step 4. The surprising-service activities and the team's methodology of improving customer satisfaction are reinforced.

Measure of Success

In the systems circle the customer experiences the quality of products and services as output of the operational-level processes affected by continuous improvement processes at the TQM triad level. Here in the people circle, a parallel experience exists. The customer experiences the quality of customer service as the output of the operational level processes affected by customer satisfaction processes at the TQM triad level. In both cases, pre-TQM, there existed products and services that met customers' requirements and customer service that met customers' expectations. With the TQM triad level added, a new dimension of quality is possible. Products and services now predictably meet customers' requirements produced by systems that are continuously decreasing their poor cost of quality and continuously improving their performance. Customer service now is aimed at surprising the customer to produce not just a satisfied but a delighted customer.

The following is an example operational definition for quality customer service that delights the customer.

1. *Define the characteristic to be measured.* The quality of the organization's customer service including the expected and surprising elements.
2. *Choose a measurement device.* A customer service survey form measuring effects from both elements.
3. *Describe the method for measurement.*
   a. Form a focus group from your customer base.
   b. Work with the focus group to develop the list of expected customer service activities.
   c. Design questions to monitor these activities.
   d. Design questions to capture information about surprising customer service occurrences.
   e. Administer the survey to a sample of your customers.
   f. Use histograms to build graphical presentations of the results for each question.
   g. Resurvey every six months or every quarter.
4. *State the decision criteria for evaluation of the resulting measurements.* Plot the results on a chart to indicate the average and spread of the data from survey period to survey period. Watch for statistically significant trends indicating that the customer service is generating higher customer satisfaction. Individual questions that do not show positive trends can be forwarded to the quality steering committee or a CQI team for action.

Customer Surveys

Be cautious about placing too much emphasis on survey results. Managing a business with survey results has been characterized as driving while looking only in the rearview mirror. Information is available in survey results to drive continuous improvement, but it's practically useless for strategic planning. The development of innovative strategies in the direction circle gains little useful information for the future direction of the organization from customer surveys about past performance.

In the terminology of the TQM triad, customer surveys are an intercircle communication tool between People and Systems.

Surveys are a valid source of ideas for continuous improvement projects. They may help you discover previously unknown problems or assist in prioritizing problems. CQI teams may employ surveys to test the acceptance of certain corrective actions that may have an effect on customer satisfaction.

Surveys and the Seven Basic Tools

What do we do with all these survey data? This question is one more reason everyone in the organization should understand and use the seven basic tools. The raw data need to be transformed into useful process information to provide individuals, managers, and teams with the knowledge to make informed decisions. This starts with the ability to be able to construct a survey that will allow for the transformation to occur. Garbage in will always yield garbage out.

An important concern is the discrimination of the rating system in the survey. Giving the customer a range of possible responses from 1 to 10 will allow you to acquire data that will be useful for two purposes: comparing survey results to earlier surveys and identifying areas that need CQI action. If your only focus in doing a customer survey is to identify problem areas, this rating system need not be followed. Survey questions that require yes/no, did not meet/met/exceeded, or 1-to-5 rating responses will adequately point you to areas that need attention.

Simple data reduction and presentation of the results are usually the best. For example, very little is added to the understanding of the survey results when they are presented in terms of their standard deviation. Most of us that are involved in CQI don't think in terms of that statistical value. A graphical presentation of the data by constructing a histogram of the results, in conjunction with the calculated average, will give the CQI team useful information from the survey data.

Balancing the Training

The compelling need to provide teams with large doses of training in people-circle techniques should be examined and possibly checked. For example, training in consensus building or conflict resolution may be needed to allow a CQI team to function effectively, but first the team members need to be conversant in the seven basic tools and CQI methodology. Often a misguided team diagnosis is made when it's decided the team can't work well together in the CQI process, when the fact is that the team can't work the process. Teams that get along so well that members want to hug each other but can't tell a control chart from a flowchart will only solve problems that can be eliminated with a dose of sweetness.

The people circle offers many opportunities for employee improvement. A caution worth stating: Do not go overboard when looking over the smorgasbord of selections. If 85 percent of the problems or opportunities for improvement are systems related, and this number is probably conservative, why do so many organizations spend so much of their resources on solving people problems? Could it be that we still like to blame someone instead of questioning the systems? Granted, employees are part of the system, but too often the training approach would lead an observer to perceive that people *are* the system.

 **Chapter 7**

The Circle Interactions

Introduction

Viable TQM systems rely partially on the interactions between the triad circles. These interactions are reflected in the model as overlaps of the circles. Some are attributes of processes that naturally occur but are not the primary reason for the processes' implementation, and others depend on the implementation of special programs specifically to gain the advantages of the interactions. Whether these interactions occur naturally or through thoughtful strategies, they are important constituents of the TQM system. An example of a naturally occurring interaction would be a CQI project that eliminated errors in an order-filling process to produce continuous improvement, and, consequently, because of the error-free process, customer satisfaction improved. An example of a program specifically implemented to cause a positive interaction between two circles would be the cost-of-quality process measurement tool that provides communication between the systems and direction circles.

There exists a dependency relationship between the circles that must not be neglected. This dependency is present with each pair of circles, and care given to nurturing and growing it greatly enhances the overall outcomes of the unified TQM approach.

Circle Overlaps: Added Benefits of a Quality Process

Most programs, when implemented, will produce added benefits through interactions with the other two circles. The benefits might be (1) from synergism with a process in another circle, (2) from contributory effects on another circle's process, or (3) from activities driven by process actions in another circle. These benefits should be expected and planned for when a quality program is implemented.

Synergism Between Processes in Different Circles

Combinations of processes in the people and systems circles offer many examples of synergistic activity. Team-building training, developing listening and communication skills, and empowering employees to manage their own processes are all resident processes in the people circle that contribute to the generation of internal and external customer satisfaction. These same processes also enhance the CQI process in the systems circle to produce improved results from CQI team projects.

Facilitating CQI project teams for maximum performance will ensure the development of the intercircle synergism. An example of a new team being formed will illustrate this point. Many organizations will have the genesis of their CQI teams in the steering committee, which is usually composed of upper managers. The Valley Clinic steering committee determined the need for a team to redesign the process of gathering patient information at registration at the beginning of each patient visit. The present process was not uniform from one nurse to the next, and vital information was often missing or inaccurate. Their first two major steps in the CQI process were to select the team members and then train them in the use of the seven basic tools and the problem-solving process. The problem-solving process gave the team a structured approach for using the seven basic tools in identifying root causes, defining corrective actions, and implementing the solution. The Valley Clinic CQI team was guided through this process by Neill, the quality director, acting as the facilitator conversant in the use of the seven basic tools and problem-solving process. New teams suffer from problems relative to the tools that mature teams no longer experience, and the facilitator must be able to recognize what is occurring and take proper action.

Neill provided just-in-time training for the seven-step problem-solving process the clinic had adopted, introducing certain of the seven basic tools as they applied to the process. He noticed that with the training and facilitation the team was seemingly effective in working on the CQI project, but problems were still present in team meetings. Certain team members were attempting to take over the agenda, and others were not communicating well. This is the time to bring in training from the people circle. Team-building and listening skills training was provided to the CQI team to improve individual's interactions. The Valley Clinic CQI team was now able to reach optimal performance with the synergism between the problem-solving process and the people-circle skills training.

An important point here is the need to have the primary process, in this case the CQI problem-solving process, operating effectively before attempting to gain the synergism from interacting with an overlapping circle's process. Far too many attempts have been made to improve a team's performance by team-building or similar type training when the real flaw was with seven basic tools competency.

***Triad Theorem 17: To gain the full advantage
of synergism between processes,
each process must be operating effectively.***

Contributory Effects in Another Circle

In addition to synergism, the overlap symbolizes that a process in any circle also contributes to the outcomes of the other two circles. Let's return to the CQI process in Systems for an example.

The 4-Star Hotel housekeeping CQI team had as its project goal a significant reduction in time spent in preparing rooms for guests. Presently guests are not experiencing any delays in checking in; hence, the time savings would be an economic advantage for the hotel with no noticeable effect on the guests. This, at least, was the initial reasoning of the CQI team members. So the payoff would be continuous improvement benefits with a corresponding increase in growth potential.

After working through the project, an innovative solution was proposed. The housekeepers decided to clean rooms as a three-member team, instead of one housekeeper per room. The next step was a pilot run of the new process on one floor of the hotel. One team member removed the used linen and towels, while the second started cleaning the bath and the third vacuumed the carpet. While the second housekeeper continued with cleaning the bath, the other two made the bed or beds and replenished the room supplies. Not only was the work more enjoyable as a team, but they discovered that they could prepare rooms using 10 percent less labor than with the old process. The team considered the pilot a success, fully implemented the new process, and disbanded the CQI team.

Management had been monitoring the level of complaints received from guests calling the front desk and also from the guest survey forms placed in each room. They noticed that after implementation of the housekeeping team concept, the complaints concerning room preparation or missing bath supplies dropped by 73 percent. The CQI project had a contributory effect on customer satisfaction in addition to the continuous improvement effect. The facilitator of the CQI project team documented these surprise results by adding an estimate to their cost-of-quality savings total for the 73 percent drop in error rate.

One Process, Three Outcomes. In general, TQM processes generating continuous improvement and TQM processes generating customer satisfaction will in turn generate growth potential. This is one of the main reasons that upper management in the direction circle deemed it worthwhile to implement the TQM system. This is the strategic planning process of the direction circle coming full circle.

Additionally, processes that generate continuous improvement many times have unexpected (as in the preceding example) or sometimes expected effects on customer satisfaction. A CQI team should be watchful for these effects, understand why they happened, and document them in project records. After discovery, an effort needs to be made by the CQI team to ensure that the activities producing the effects become a permanent part of the solution.

The power of the CQI process on the TQM system can be illustrated with the triad-model circle terminology (see Figure 7.1). The observant reader may note the similarity to Deming's (1986) famous chain reaction that starts with improved quality and ends with providing more jobs.

Activities Driven by Process Actions in Another Circle

This is possibly the most neglected of the three interactions. When this interaction is missing, it can be characterized as either a breakdown in communication between circles or a missing supporting process. These driven activities do not automatically take place when a certain key process action occurs in another circle. A viable TQM system must be in place to take advantage

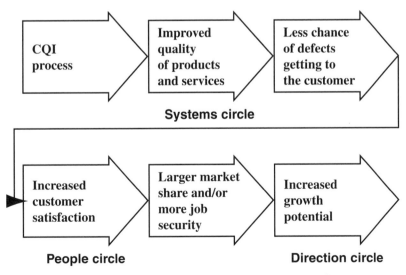

Figure 7.1: CQI affects outcomes in all three circles.

of the opportunities presented by this interaction. Examples abound in the area of customer satisfaction surveys or customer complaints collected in the people circle, but with no follow-up activities occurring in the systems circle.

Organizations train frontline personnel to take great care of the guests, customers, or clients when they voice a service complaint or want to return a product. Frequently, however, the follow-up activity to ensure the complaint-causing service error or nonconforming product never happens again doesn't occur.

An experience in a restaurant recently reminded me of the fallacy of focusing on customer satisfaction at all costs and neglecting continuous improvement, hence missing the opportunity to gain the benefit of the interaction. My order of blackened salmon was of such extremely poor quality that a steak knife was needed to cut the filet. When the waitress returned to inquire about the salmon, I indicated my displeasure. She very quickly offered to replace it. Good customer service move, right? When I told her I was rushed and couldn't wait for another meal preparation, she offered a dessert, on the house. Well, that I could not pass up.

Many service organizations consider such a situation as customer service actions and regard this empowerment of their employees to "make things right" as their total quality management program. If this emphasis on quickly correcting errors is the TQM focus, their efforts are doomed and profits are being adversely affected. The action of replacing the meal or providing a free dessert is classified as a quick fix. By definition, a *quick fix* is a temporary solution to an ongoing problem to prevent short-term process failure. They are needless expenses and are categorized as failure costs of poor quality. Quick fixes are a necessary step in problem solving, but many times they are mistaken as permanent solutions. An organization may actually budget for this rework to legitimize or rationalize the quick-fix action.

While enjoying my "free" dessert, I wondered what activities were driven by this error occurrence. Did the error get recorded on a data sheet for later transfer to a control chart? Was the type of failure recorded for later analysis with a Pareto chart?

Did anyone really care about eliminating the chances of this error occurring in the future? True customer satisfaction in this scenario derives from an understanding that an organization is taking steps to permanently eliminate problems and really is serious about prevention. This is the difference between creating a customer who simply walks out satisfied and one who will want to return, knowing the next experience will be improved.

Restaurants aren't the only businesses missing the opportunity; it's also widespread in retail establishments. Upon returning a defective light fixture to a local outlet for a national building-supply retailer, I found the customer service in refunding the purchase price was fast, efficient, and friendly. The clerk, however, seemed to not care whether I had simply changed my mind on the purchase or whether it was a defective product. I waited for the inquiry—it didn't come. Everything returned is placed back into inventory unless it's obviously defective or broken. How many times will that light fixture be sold and returned before it's finally taken out of circulation? The supplier of this fixture to the retailer will probably never hear of the problem. No chance for the problem to ever be solved permanently, just quick fixes ad infinitum to supposedly keep customer satisfaction levels high. An opposite effect is happening where customers are realizing that the quality can't be trusted, so they are leaving in droves.

Triad Theorem 18: Excellent customer service while righting a wrong, not followed and supported by continuous improvement, is no more than an expensive quick fix.

Communication Between the Circles

In addition to the added benefits contributed by process interactions between circles, benefits are also generated by the inter-circle communications tools. Two major tools will be discussed: COQ, a link between Systems and Direction; and open-book management (OBM), a link between People and Direction. You may have other TQM communications tools that can be placed in the unified total quality model, and certainly more will be developed that will add to the effectiveness of the TQM system. Another powerful intercircle communication tool, hoshin planning, will be discussed in chapter 8.

The traditional communication between management and staff has been monthly status reports and yearly performance reviews, both tools of the operational level. When an attempt is made to apply these tools at the TQM triad level, however, they fail to support the effective operation of TQM processes. Management has a need to know what these processes are doing for the organization. Cost of quality transmits that information from the CQI teams to management. Staff members who are running the organization's processes, maintaining the systems, and implementing continuous improvement and customer satisfaction methodologies have a need to know what effects they are having on the organization's fiscal health. OBM transmits that information from management to the staff (see Figure 7.2).

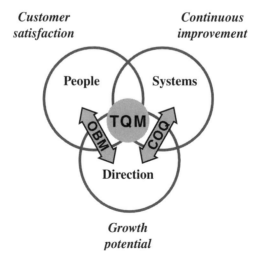

Figure 7.2: *Intercircle communication tools at the triad level: Open-book management (OBM) and cost of quality (COQ).*

Cost of Quality

The third and fourth quality cost categories, the costs of internal and external failure—many times labeled the costs of nonconformance or the cost of poor quality—are of interest in this discussion of communication between Systems and Direction. Three significant benefits are derived from the use of the cost of quality to monitor the improvement processes.

1. The true impact of a problem can be understood.
2. CQI projects can be prioritized.
3. Dollars saved by CQI projects can be documented.

All three communicate valuable decision-making information to management. Knowing the impact of a problem often will create a sense of urgency in dealing with its permanent elimination and not continuing to quick fix the errors. Most organizations will have more problem-solving or continuous improvement projects than available team resources. The ability to logically prioritize the candidate projects provides a useful management aid. Finally, the tabulation of COQ savings by CQI teams in dollars provides powerful proof of the value of TQM and specifically continuous improvement. Management will not question the value of the TQM effort when the cost-of-quality savings is proving that a significant payback is being generated.

As an example of cost of quality in use, let's return to the 4-Star Hotel's CQI team project. The team ended with a savings of 10 percent on labor costs and a decline in complaints on room preparation and missing bath supplies of 73 percent. Table 7.1 translates the percentages into total potential savings per week.

When the 10 percent labor savings and the COQ savings from the 73 percent reduction in complaints were documented by the CQI team, were the savings being generated? Not yet. It needs to be communicated to management, and then management must take the correct action to capture the results measured by the teams (see Figure 7.3).

Table 7.1: *4-Star Hotel housekeeping CQI team COQ report.*

Assumptions

Staff:	20 housekeepers
Wages and benefits:	$10 per hour
Work week:	40 hours
Cleaning rate:	1 room per hour

All costs and calculations on a per-week basis.

Total labor costs:
20 housekeepers × 40 hours × $10 per hour = $8000

Total rooms cleaned:
20 housekeepers × 40 hours × 1 room per hour = 800 rooms

Total receipts:
800 rooms × $100 per room = $80,000

Complaint call information:
80 complaints per week, 60 called in, 40 missing-item calls

Item	Calculation	Failure COQ	Potential savings
1	10% savings in labor costs × $8000 =		$800
2	Time on phone: 60 calls × 2 minutes (.033 hours) × $10 =	20	
3	Delivering missing items: 40 × 10 minutes (.167 hours) × $10 =	67	
4	Recleaning rooms: 5 per week × 1 hour × $10 =	50	
5	Discounts given to dissatisfied customers: 40 rooms × $20 =	800	
	Total failure COQ	$937	
	73 percent savings ($937 × .73)		684
	Total potential savings per week		$1484

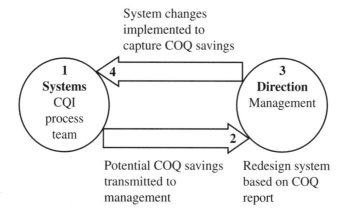

Figure 7.3: *The four-step process to gain COQ improvements.*

What usually happens when CQI project teams give presentations to management doesn't look like Figure 7.3. The deviations, possibly serious flaws, are of two types: (1) no communications device like COQ exists between Systems and Direction, and/or (2) no systems changes are directed by management.

No COQ Communication. One main cause of CQI failure is no proof of improvement. No proof leads to management not seeing any payback. Interest is soon lost in the process, and it's on to the next buzzword program. Many organizations overlook the importance of communicating to management the savings potential of the in-process CQI projects in dollars. A strong signal that this exists where you work would be team reports couched in language such as "this project reduced the production error rate by 7.4 percent," "on-time-delivery has improved from 86 percent to 94 percent," or "manufacturing scrap has been reduced by 76 percent." Percentages don't have the impact of thousands of dollars, and the percentage figures miss many of the cost-of-quality factors. In fact, the percentages hide valuable information that management needs in order to capture the savings predicted by CQI project teams. Which commands more attention: "Our team reduced complaints by 73 percent," or "our team reduced quality costs due to complaints by $35,568 per year"?

No System Changes. Your team reports to management that the total potential savings for the housekeeping project is $77,168 per year (see Table 7.1). Management applauds your effort, makes sure the team gets recognition in the next company newsletter, and focuses its attention on the next problem in a seemingly never-ending series. If management doesn't make the necessary systems changes, how much of the reported potential savings will actually be realized? Probably only the *discount given* amount of $30,368 ($800 × 73 percent × 52 weeks = $30,368) will be captured. What happened to the other $46,800 of predicted savings? That part of the savings requires systems changes to be designed and implemented by management. The *how* of this effort will be discussed in chapter 8. Suffice it to say that without the Systems–Direction communication using the COQ tool and follow-up action by management in the direction circle, TQM will likely wither from lack of expected performance. Management has no time for programs that do not enhance the bottom line, and rightly so.

Open-Book Management

As the cost-of-quality tool is a driving force behind getting management committed to process improvement and the TQM philosophy, open-book management is a driving force behind getting staff commitment to participate on CQI team projects.

> *Open-book management:* Providing staff access to and understanding of company financial statements to reveal how actions, changes, and decisions in subsystems affect the goals of the overall system measured by standard accounting procedures.

At the TQM triad level, open-book management provides the connection between cost-of-quality savings and the resultant effects on the organization's expenses and profit margin. This is necessary because COQ is a nonstandard accounting procedure of the TQM triad level that must be linked to the standard accounting procedures of the operational level. OBM has important applications at the operational level also, but we are interested here in its TQM applications.

An organization's staff usually has little if any experience in constructing or reading financial statements. Employees will need some education in the terminology of profit margin, net profit, gross profit, and expenses; also, how does this all come together so the business can actually make money? More specifically, how will the efforts of process, quality, and customer service improvement affect the bottom line of the financial statement?

One powerful insight to be gained from OBM techniques that will certainly promote the importance of CQI teams can be illustrated by returning to our 4-Star Hotel project. The housekeeping CQI team was satisfied with the outcomes from its project, but after hearing that weekly receipts for the hotel averaged $80,000, the team's savings of $1484 seemed insignificant. Open-book management training changed team members' perspective on the value of their efforts. The housekeepers learned about net profit—what was left from receipts after all expenses had been paid. For the 4-Star Hotel, net profit was 5 percent of receipts or $4000 per week. They also learned that if management could change the systems to capture the entire cost savings from their CQI project, the $1484 would become additional net profit. That was a much more exciting comparison: Their project had the potential of increasing net profit by 37 percent.

The new knowledge gained from management opening up the hotel's financial records allowed one more interesting comparison. The hotel charged, on an average, $100 for the standard suite. This meant that each room contributed $5 to the net profit. If the team's savings was divided by that $5 per room net profit, the result indicated it was the equivalent to the net profit from more than 296 rooms. Wow! This little project could make the hotel as much net profit as renting out 296 more rooms per week. The team had accomplished something the reservations and marketing department couldn't even dream of as a goal. They felt like heroes. Needless to say, management was already planning the next CQI project.

The knowledge gained by employees trained in the basics of financial analysis changes their perspective on the importance of process improvement. If the waitress serving my blackened salmon had known her employer's net profit margin was 10 percent, she could have calculated the loss to the restaurant's net profit from giving away food. Understanding that the restaurant would have to sell 10 more meals to cover the loss of giving away one meal is a powerful fact that is unknown without the use of open-book techniques. With the financial facts known, quick fixes are seen as being a very expensive way to maintain customer satisfaction, and the true value of process improvement is obvious.

Communication Links Between the People and Systems Circles

Since the definition for quality in the systems circle relies on meeting customers' requirements and a driver for CQI is customer feedback, communication certainly is required between the customer's voice in the people circle and the activities in the systems circle at both the TQM triad level and operational level. The requirements check as an activity of the systems circle whose primary objective is to establish two-way communication between the customer and supplier was discussed in chapter 5. Customer surveys, supplying customer feedback to the systems circle, were positioned in the people circle in chapter 6.

Both the requirements check and customer survey share a common attribute in practice. They tend to be used by CQI teams working on process improvement or problem-elimination projects. Using them to drive the development of customer-focused products and services doesn't appear to be their popular use. Is there a methodology that will cause this communication between the customer and supplier very early in the product and service development process?

Communication Between the TQM Triad and Operational Levels

Quality function deployment (QFD) is one answer to the preceding question.

> *Quality function deployment:* A method of carrying the voice of the customer all the way through the design/ development/production process (Melum and Collett 1995, 81).

The QFD methodology is a major information pipeline between the customer and all three circles of the operational level. Representatives from marketing, design, production, and sales directly communicate with customer representatives to gain a thorough understanding of their needs, expectations, and perceptions. The outcome is more apt to be a new product or service that meets or exceeds the customers' needs as originally designed and produced.

Certain tools, activities, and methodologies resident in their prescribed circles at the TQM triad level can operate on the processes in all three circles at the operational level to produce measurable results attributable to TQM. For example, the operational-level processes of customer retention (People), order fulfillment (Systems), and new product development (Direction) could all be radically redesigned with reengineering (Direction), improved with CQI (Systems), or made more customer friendly (People). These are interactions that start in one circle at the TQM triad level and interact with a process in a different circle at the operational level. They follow similar interaction cycles to those discussed in chapters 4, 5, and 6, but they involve different combinations of circles—for example, the direction circle at the TQM triad level with the systems circle at the operational level. When reengineering from the direction circle is applied to the operational-level process of order fulfillment, both service quality and profit quality are improved. This in turn would produce increased growth potential, continuous improvement, and customer satisfaction.

Balancing the Circles

People and Systems Balance

The balance of concern here is between the people and systems circles. With a balanced implementation approach that includes the quality techniques, tools, activities, and methodologies from each circle, success of the TQM initiative can't be guaranteed; but it does greatly improve the probability of success. An organization's TQM system will be its own uniquely designed balance of the People and Systems components. This is not a one-size-fits-all model.

The tendency for an organization to take on a certain balance is usually traceable to its traditional pre-TQM balance at the operational level. A service business will favor the people circle and a manufacturing company will tend toward the systems circle, because that is where they are the most comfortable. This preexisting balance may affect the way an organization formulates its quality initiative. An adjustment of this formulation based on an understanding of the relationships, dynamics, and interactions of the TQM triad may be needed to develop a viable TQM system.

Mega-Mart Inc. was just starting its total quality efforts. Management had chosen this strategy in an attempt to improve sales and profits from last year's lackluster performance. Customer service had always been the forte of the organization, but if doing it better was the answer, they were ready to commit the required resources for the training and implementation. One year and $40,000 worth of customer service training later, there seemed to be no discernable change in the financial numbers. The customer satisfaction survey given one year ago compared with the one just completed did indicate a slight positive shift, so all was not lost.

Jan, the vice president of sales, had been doing some thinking about attempting a continuous quality improvement program—it did seem to work in the assembly plant where her husband worked. This time there would be no training-for-all approach. Two teams of seven employees were chosen to pilot the experiment.

Four months later, the effort did seem to be producing some results. This cost-of-quality tool the team was using did allow management to see the bottom-line gain, which admittedly would have been hidden by normal variation in sales and profit figures. The two teams were excitedly going after process problems where before the employees hadn't even recognized processes. Customer satisfaction was not suffering either; it was continuing its upward trend.

Balancing with Order

There is an order of implementation for some of the TQM programs. It's a little difficult to empower employees without first training and ensuring competence in the seven basic tools and process management skills. That would be like throwing a teenager the family car keys without first having him or her attend a driver training course.

Another similar example of ordered programs is the combination of the CQI problem-solving process and team-building skills. Teams that first become conversant with a formal problem-solving approach can then be observed for any signals that may indicate a need for an intervention to produce effective team interactions. Are team members having trouble with confrontational behavior? Can they reach consensus when required? Are they having trouble communicating? In this example there are cases where a team's understanding of the problem-solving approach can eliminate the need for training in team-building skills. When a CQI team understands that the correct use of the cause-and-effect diagram is to capture all the common causes affecting the process and not just to find one singular root cause, many of the arguments and confrontations that normally would occur are eliminated. The team members perceive that they don't have to defend their favorite root cause; instead, they work together to develop corrective actions to eliminate or reduce the effects of a group of root causes.

Chapter 8

Making the Model Work for You

Introduction

There are those who say that TQM is a necessary passport to doing business in today's world. Not so. At least the studies don't show this. Three studies cited by Shapiro (1995) indicate that few organizations have seen a payoff from their quality efforts. Therefore, we can hardly say it's a requirement for doing business in the 1990s.

Total quality management is still, as it always has been, a way to differentiate your organization from the competition. When you're successful in the implementation of your TQM system, the payoff will be very worthwhile. The TQM system offers your organization payoffs in three areas: continuous improvement, customer satisfaction, and growth potential. All result in bottom-line rewards. TQM remains a powerful competitive device.

Interconnecting the Circles

One of the benefits of using the unified total quality model is the development and implementation of interrelated total quality strategies. Gone will be the discontinuity caused by fad-of-the-year programs. With the interconnecting of methodologies, techniques, activities, and tools, the TQM system begins to take meaningful shape.

Another aspect of the interrelationship of the model components is the compatibility created in the decisions, understanding, and actions by managers, teams, and individuals.

Individuals will understand the bottom-line effects of defective products and services. They'll see the economic folly in offering customer service at all costs to placate an unhappy customer when there is no follow-up action to ensure that the problem never occurs again. Individuals will be motivated to take action, redesigning processes and actively participating on CQI teams.

Teams will understand the high cost of working in processes that cause nonconformances. They will be able to communicate this cost to management and offer long-term corrective actions.

Managers will understand the vicious cycle of high employee turnover and low customer satisfaction. They will be able to work with CQI teams in gaining the highest possible payoff from improvement projects.

So Many Programs, So Little Time

Whether your organization is just now deciding to enter the total quality world or you have decided not to renew your membership in the TQM fad-of-the-year club, one big question remains. You see the whole picture now in the TQM triad, but is there an order of implementation for all these methodologies, activities, and tools? There are many guides available to help with this potentially overwhelming task. These aren't models so much as stepwise procedures or programs to effectively implement, in a thoughtful sequence, the many available options. None will cover all the methodologies, activities, and tools represented in the unified total quality model, but they are effective in adding needed structure to the implementation process and producing quality results.

These stepwise programs range from simple problem-solving approaches—which offer guidance in the selection of which tool to use and how to use it — to the complex implementation of major TQM constituent systems — which may include many supporting methodologies. The following discussion will address one of the more complex programs.

Hoshin Planning

There are many definitions and descriptions in the literature for hoshin planning because each organization designs and defines the basic concept to fit its own needs. I've selected a few to assist us in the study of how hoshin planning relates to the TQM triad.

> Hoshin planning is a system. It is a component of the TQM system that allows an organization to plan and execute strategic organizational breakthrough. (GOAL/QPC 1990, 10)

> Global goals, which are the total quality objectives, are deployed to all sectors and departments within the company. (Kelada 1996, 354)

Hoshin planning is a powerful process to drive breakthrough improvements in key operational-level systems to meet strategic quality objectives for the year. Note that the first definition labels hoshin planning as a component of TQM. If it's a component of TQM, then we should be able to position it in the unified total quality model. Hoshin planning can be one of the main information carriers from the direction circle at the TQM triad level to the operational-level people and systems circles. This is reinforced by Melum and Collett (1995, 17) in calling hoshin planning "the vertical component of total quality management. It is the compass that sets the major direction for the organization's TQM efforts for everyone from the CEO to the front-line employee." The following direction circle activities are the first steps in the hoshin planning process: (1) development of an organization's vision, (2) long-term strategic quality planning, and (3) defining objectives for the upcoming year. The next step of communicating the objectives to all departments within the organization moves the process to the other two circles.

The objectives derived from the earlier steps in the hoshin planning process will focus on key operational systems and processes that must be improved to cause breakthrough. The continuous improvement interaction cycles of the TQM triad discussed in chapters 5 and 6 (see Figure 5.3 on page 94 and Figure 6.2 on page 108) illustrate the dynamics that will actually produce the improvement and resultant breakthrough.

Hoshin planning also drives the use of the 7 MP tools (see chapter 4) and the analysis of data using the seven basic tools. The 7 MP tools are valuable assets to the hoshin planning process. They are "indispensable in surfacing breakthrough ideas out of chaos and converting them into implementable plans" (GOAL/QPC 1990, 12). In the context of the TQM triad, hoshin planning relies on the analysis of data from customers (People) and processes (Systems) to assist managers in the direction circle to form strategic quality plans leading to breakthrough.

Hoshin Planning and Management by Objectives

Comparing these two programs provides some insight into the workings of the TQM triad and the differences between the programs. Objectives developed by most organizations' management by objectives (MBO) processes are rather pedestrian: Increase sales by 10 percent, bring two new products to market, or increase market share by 5 percent. MBO, as usually practiced, emphasizes incremental improvement results of operational processes. Hoshin planning, on the other hand, emphasizes breakthrough, listening to the customer, using the quality tools, utilizing the team approach, and process/systems thinking.

The main difference between the two processes with similar activity steps is the starting point of each in the TQM triad and the interaction with the circles at the TQM triad level. MBO starts in the direction circle at the operational level and communicates objectives to the people and systems circles at the operational level. No interaction or even any recognition of the TQM triad level occurs. Hoshin planning starts in the direction circle at the TQM triad level and then communicates objectives to the people and systems circles at the operational level. At this point, interaction of the TQM triad level systems with the operational level becomes an integral part of the hoshin planning process.

Internal and External Consultants

In the following sections the term *consultant* also implies trainer or facilitator, anyone assigned or hired to provide assistance in the TQM effort.

Internal Consultants

One of the positive trends in total quality is the proliferation of staff positions with the title quality improvement consultant. A TQM system built on the internal expertise of an organization backed by the total commitment of management is well on its way to success. Success in total quality requires intimate knowledge of the organization—its structure, history, culture, and work habits. These attributes cannot be easily or accurately divined by an outsider.

Let's put this in the context of the TQM triad. Two paradigms that seem to lock up some minds is "We are different; that won't work here" and "We are a service organization; that only works in manufacturing." In actuality, the differences are at the operational level, and no one would argue that; but at the TQM triad level the methodologies, tools, and techniques are the same. The TQM implementation becomes (1) learn the methodologies in the TQM triad level and (2) apply them to your operational-level processes. An organization can get external assistance for the first step, but step 2 is really best handled by the internal quality improvement consultants. The blending of the TQM processes with the organization's operational processes is the rightful responsibility of the internal consultant.

External Consultants

An external consultant, according to the previous discussion, can have a major role in assisting with building the TQM triad level expertise for the organization. Certainly part of this assistance would want to be demonstrations of TQM applications to operations based on the organization's own real-world processes.

Here are some guidelines for selecting an external consultant based on the TQM triad.

1. *Select a consultant with expertise in the circle where you've determined a need for training or consulting.* Be cautious of someone who claims to be a TQM consultant. The bodies of knowledge represented by the three circles are too incredibly large and diverse for one person to claim expertise in all components. Consultants may not identify with one of the circles, but understanding their offerings and questioning philosophies will allow you to place them within the model. There can be subdivisions of expertise within circles. For instance, a consultant with proficiency in customer service surveys may not be a good choice for team-building skills training, although both are resident in the people circle.

A related caution: Be wary of the snake-oil methodology promoter who promises to give your organization everything needed for all three circles of the TQM triad in one package.

2. *Be aware of redundancies in People and Systems programs.* If your organization has implemented a formal problem-solving process as part of the CQI process, watch for possible duplication in later training. People-circle consultants will usually base their team-building, facilitator, or consensus-building training on a problem-solving model — make sure it's the model your organization is already using in the systems circle. The trainer should be expected to adapt his or her techniques to your process, not the other way around. Introducing a second problem-solving process is redundant, at the least, and can be quite disruptive to the quality systems already in place. Teams struggling with the application of a still-unfamiliar procedure don't enjoy being hit with another duplicative procedure.

Change will be occurring quite rapidly in a TQM implementation. We don't need to add nonproductive change to the effort. Internal consultants managing these seemingly trivial matters can eliminate wasted organizational energy and resources spent on change that isn't essential.

On the other hand, leaders of evolving TQM processes should be constantly searching for new techniques that can improve their present processes. Continuous improvement of the TQM system is worthwhile—it's the unplanned and unexpected apparent replacement of techniques that is counterproductive.

3. *When searching for assistance with the systems-circle methodologies and tools, ASQC certified quality engineer certification should be a required item on the internal or external consultant's resume.* This is no guarantee for success, but it does help to prevent you from hiring someone who believes attending a three-day seminar on SPC makes him or her an expert on the subject.

ISO 9000 and the Unified Total Quality Model

Quality processes and systems resident in the TQM triad level are the most effective when supported by and interacting with strong operational-level quality processes and systems. Is there anything that can guide an organization in building consistently strong operational-level processes and systems?

ISO 9000 series standards are guides for developing a quality assurance system. "Their use contributes to the consistency and coherence of conformity assessment worldwide," according to Roger Frost (1996), ISO Central Secretariat, in Geneva, Switzerland. Organizations that model their operational-level quality assurance systems after one of the three standards— ISO 9001, ISO 9002, or ISO 9003—develop a strong basis for interaction among all six circles of the extended TQM triad (see Figure 8.1).

First, the three circles at the operational level require an effective quality assurance system to facilitate communication between the departments of the organization. Management (direction circle) communicates its quality policy. The organization's people interacting with customers communicate requirements to Systems. Section by section through the standard, requirements are defined that establish interactions among the

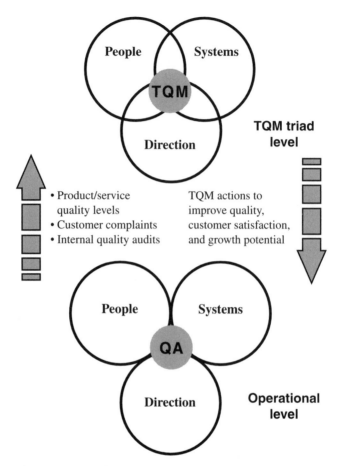

Figure 8.1: *Quality assurance and total quality interactions.*

circles, whether it is contract review, design control, data control, purchasing, process control, or quality audits.

Second, the TQM systems interact with the quality assurance systems to gain useful information about product and service quality levels, customer complaints, and internal quality audits to drive continuous improvement, customer satisfaction, and growth potential.

TQM systems don't require a quality assurance system based on the ISO 9000 series standards, but the standards do provide a strong foundation. Conversely, having an ISO-based quality assurance system does not by any stretch of the imagination cause a TQM system to materialize, any more than buying the latest in measurement gages and setting up a machined parts inspection system would cause SPC to automatically develop.

I appreciate the intentions of those who promote or are able to use the ISO 9000 series quality system guidelines as a route to TQM, but we must separate good intentions from hard facts. When we are not precise in defining what a quality assurance system does for an organization, we generate misunderstanding among quality neophytes or managers looking for "the easy way to do TQM." These people misinterpret the good intentions as meaning a quality assurance system based on ISO 9000 guidelines is all an organization needs. Actually it's just the first step in a long journey.

Section 4.14 in ISO 9001, corrective and preventive action, is a good place to forge a major connection with the TQM system. If a TQM system is not in place and ready to support this section, too much emphasis is usually placed on conformance rather than on continuous quality improvement. One of the following actions usually occurs when a problem is discovered in a product or service: (1) a new procedure is written, (2) workers are advised to follow the existing procedure, or (3) more training is ordered. With a TQM system in place, the problem discovery may drive the formation of a CQI team to formulate corrective and preventive actions that will be effective for the long term.

The Baldrige Award and the Unified Total Quality Model

The Baldrige Award criteria could be thought of as a structured diagnostic tool for the assessment of an organization's unified approach to TQM implementation. I use the term *unified* because the Baldrige Award criteria not only addresses continuous improvement (Systems), but also customer satisfaction (People) and business results (Direction). The criteria assess the outcomes of all three TQM triad circles, which indicates the compatibility of the criteria and the unified total quality model.

Another method to illustrate the relationship of the Baldrige Award criteria and the unified total quality model is to employ the PDCA cycle. *Plan* a TQM system based on the understanding of the interrelationship of methodologies, activities, and tools gained from the model. *Do*—implement the plan by building your organization's TQM system. *Check* the implementation results by using the criteria as an assessment tool. *Act* on the information gained from the assessment. What needs to be revised in or added to the TQM system to raise the next Baldrige Award criteria assessment score?

In the previous section it was stated that the ISO 9000 series standards are models for developing a quality assurance system at the operational level. Where those standards assisted an organization in developing quality assurance interactions between circles and within circles at the operational level (see Figure 8.1), the Baldrige Award criteria, through assessment and the resulting guidance for improvement, assists an organization in building a TQM system that effectively addresses all six circles of the extended TQM triad.

The Baldrige Award Criteria and Continuous Improvement

The Baldrige Award criteria state that continuous improvement, whether it be incremental or breakthrough, needs "to be 'embedded' in the way the company operates" (NIST 1997, 39). A constant and consistent theme runs through the Baldrige Award criteria of requesting documentation on how processes and systems are analyzed, evaluated, and continuously improved.

Category 6, process management, addresses the key work processes of design, introduction, production, delivery, support, and supplier management. With this strong focus on processes, category 6 has a corresponding emphasis on the requirements of continuous improvement and, in general, higher process performance. A very close link with the TQM triad appears in this category of the Baldrige Award criteria. An emphasis of area 6.1b is "on how processes are improved to achieve better performance. Better performance means not only better quality

READER FEEDBACK
Fax to ASQC Quality Press Acquisitions: 414-272-1734

Comments and Areas for Improvement:
Building Your Organization's TQM System: The Unified Total Quality Model

Please give us your comments, feedback, and suggestions for making this book more useful. We believe in the importance of continuous improvement and in meeting your needs. Your comments will help determine what improvements can be made in all ASQC Quality Press books.

Please share your opinion by circling the number below:

Ratings of the book	Needs Work		Satisfactory		Excellent	Comments
Stucture, flow, and logic	1	2	3	4	5	
Content, ideas, and information	1	2	3	4	5	
Style, clarity, ease of reading	1	2	3	4	5	
Held my interest	1	2	3	4	5	
Met my overall expectations	1	2	3	4	5	

I read the book because:

The best part of the book was:

The least satisfactory part of the book was:

Other suggestions for improvement:

General comments:

Thank you for your feedback. If you do not have access to a fax machine, please mail this form to:
ASQC Quality Press, 611 East Wisconsin Avenue, P.O. Box 3005, Milwaukee, WI 53201-3005   Phone: 414-272-8575

from the customers' perspective but also better financial and operational performance—such as productivity—from the company's perspective." (NIST 1997, 28). These three types of performance are directly related to the three circles of the unified total quality model.

Operational Performance. Examples of better operational performance of processes are increased productivity, reduced rework, or reduced cycle time. Continuous improvement methodologies in the systems circle are used to improve many aspects of processes, not just the quality of products and services.

Customer-Related Performance. Better performance of this type is generated by the activities in the people circle. The customer satisfaction interaction cycle of chapter 6 improves customer-related performance by listening to customers, offering surprising service, and utilizing empowered employees; measured by customer retention, customer acquisition, and customer feedback.

Financial Performance. This area is addressed by the direction circle and its growth potential interaction cycle of chapter 4. The improvement of profit quality is one measure of better financial performance, along with traditional accounting measures such as return on investment and profitability.

The unified total quality model defines a TQM system that provides the methodologies that answer the question posed by the Baldrige Award criteria: How does the company evaluate and improve the performance of processes? This TQM system also creates a balance among customer and employee satisfaction, continuous improvement, and business results that is reflected in the Baldrige Award criteria.

The TQM Triad as a Communication Model

Three types of communication have been discussed that are present in the two-level TQM operational system: (1) dollars—

based on information from cost of quality and open book management; (2) words—based on the vision, mission, and direction circle strategies; and (3) process data—transmitting information between circles and levels. Recognizing which circle and level one is operating in and then identifying the communication interaction unique for that position can ensure total quality communication.

For example, a team working in the systems circle of the TQM triad level needs to manage customer satisfaction survey data from the people circle, COQ data for the systems and direction circles, TQM strategic information from the direction circle, and quality performance data from the operational level. Awareness of the multiple communication inputs and outputs creates an organizational efficiency not possible with monthly status reports or meetings.

Quality Training and the Triad Model

The genesis of the unified total quality model occurred when an explanation was required to assist a people-circle trainer trying to understand how CQI interacted with the material in her program. Trainers that lack the understanding of the interaction, synergism, and balance between the components of the model that are present in an effective TQM system can cause the occurrence of counterproductive activities, the most basic of which is downplaying the importance of the people circle by systems-circle trainers and the rejection of systems-circle methodologies by people-circle trainers. The dominant force in an organization, whether it be from the people or systems circles, will drive the TQM effort to an unbalanced, struggling existence and, possibly, eventual failure. This tendency can be counteracted by using the unified total quality model to plan training and implementation strategies.

Negativity in Training—Why?

When someone is learning about a new methodology, say re-engineering, and the trainer speaks negatively about other methodologies, one of three things will likely occur. (1) The trainees may have had good experiences or have some expertise with the method being discarded. They become irritated and the trainer loses credibility. (2) The trainees may have no personal experience with the methodology being rejected. The last seminar they attended was full of positive examples of what is now being "shot out of the water." Who is right? Who can be believed? (3) The last is the group of trainees caught up in the fad-of-the-year syndrome. Yes, the trainer is right—we tried that methodology and it didn't work for us either.

How much more fruitful the training would be if instructors positioned their material within the context of the unified total quality model. Building on the systems and processes that are already in place and illustrating the possible interactions would be positive and productive for the trainee and bottom-line rewarding for the organization.

The Seven Basic Tools

In chapter 5 you were asked if you thought it went unnoticed by upper management that large quantities of resources, both staff time and training budget, went into developing proficiency in the use of the tools with no apparent payoff on the bottom line.

Many failures to transfer seven basic tools training to on-the-job application are attributable to lack of attention to the direction circle contributions. This neglect starts with the decision that managers don't need the training and ends with the obvious result that they are not prepared to support the application in the systems circle. Trainers and facilitators observing the lack of training application unwittingly attempt more training for the staff, while management once again observes another quality fad that doesn't seem to be working. And we wonder why the training department takes such a hard hit during downsizing. It's really not the trainer's fault though, is it? If trained employees are sent back to the same environment they left, the training will likely be wasted. There must be a transformation of the environment to support the recently acquired training and turn it into standard practice.

Two things can be provided by management to cause the transformation: (1) facilitators with expertise in the usage of the seven basic tools and (2) a process ensuring that proper follow-up actions are taken based on knowledge gained from using the tools. Management's main objective is to make sure the training quickly nets bottom-line results. In the terminology of the TQM triad: To gain the full benefit of tools training, and for that matter any training, requires the interaction of the systems and direction circles. If this is to occur, special training will be needed by first-level managers, department heads, or shift leaders.

Traditionally these members of management have treated the tools training as something that had to be endured—a plague from the quality assurance department. The time their staff spent in the training room hurt the department's productivity numbers, and they were concerned about looking dumb when their staff asked questions about applying the new training. With the advent of self-directed work teams in some organizations, these managers felt like they were on the way out the door.

First-level managers can become a real asset to trainers by assisting in the application of the training in the workplace. As coaches or facilitators they are in a position to ensure that process operators or specially formed CQI teams deal with problems highlighted by the application of the tools. They should also be responsible for maintaining the system that utilizes the process information generated by tools usage as a major source of improvement projects. The following is a short story to demonstrate the power of first-level managers.

Ron's job wasn't being made any easier by engineering's latest design. The exotic alloys and extremely tight tolerances were not fun; in addition, management thought he should learn this new SPC stuff. He'd heard stories of this young engineer telling other machine operators how and when to adjust the cutting settings on their machines. He couldn't wait to get into this training class! Ron knew his experience on his machine, going on nine years, was all he needed to make good parts. After all, look at his scrap record. QA hadn't rejected any of his machined parts in three years, although engineering did have to admit at times that the parts would probably work with the dimension just outside the tolerance range they had selected. What could a wiggly line on a piece of chart paper tell him? If management expected him to write all these numbers down, punch a calculator, and make wiggly lines, they had better figure on hiring him a secretary.

Well, the class hadn't been too bad, it did give him a rest from those terrible tolerances, and the charting he learned wasn't difficult. He still knew that it was a useless tool for his machine, but he'd play the game. This would go away sooner or later, just like all the other quality gimmicks his company had tried.

Roger, the foreman of Ron's machining cell, was even less enthused about SPC. It seemed that changes were happening at a pace too fast for him. Implementing self-directing work teams had been especially painful. It seemed as if the company was moving to the type of machine shop where he would no longer be needed, and now they wanted him to learn statistics. In fact, when his boss had "invited" him to the training, the request seemed to have a suggestion of "or else."

Roger surprised himself—not only did he find the SPC stuff fascinating, he signed up for the additional facilitator's training. He had always been uneasy about the seemingly excessive time his machine operators spent adjusting their machines, and this control chart tool held the potential to reduce that. As an SPC facilitator he hoped he could once again feel useful and maybe even make some process improvements. The trainer had really excited him with the amount of useful machine information that the charts could display.

Roger's excitement wore off rapidly as he attempted to get the machine operators in his area to use the control charts. Why couldn't they see the importance of charting their processes? They were all going through the motions, but nothing had changed relative to their habit of machining a part, measuring it, and adjusting the machine for the next part.

Roger decided to work with one operator at a time to see if he could make a point. He realized that the machine operators had limited control chart training and couldn't be expected to see the advantages of the new tool without some assistance. Ron was his first target. Roger practically had to tie him up to keep him from fiddling with machine adjustments until the chart indicated a need to change a setting. After a week of cussing that wiggly line on the paper, Ron did have to admit to making fewer machine adjustments, and something else happened he didn't understand at all. That tight tolerance from engineering didn't seem to be quite so hard to live with now. Roger kept talking about something called *machine capability,* a concept he had learned in facilitator's training.

Ron had heard that additional training was to be offered next month. He made a mental note to talk to Roger about getting him signed up. That wiggly line did seem to help.

Contemplate what might have happened with Ron's application of training if Roger had not been there to facilitate and coach. What usually occurs then is the exercise of "train until they get it right." A sports metaphor may be apt here. No one ever became a good athlete in any sport without facilitated practice — coaching. Whether it's basketball, high jumping, or SPC, no amount of classroom training will make you proficient. Only practice and coaching will do that.

"Wait a minute," you say, "Didn't Roger become proficient with more training?" Not more proficient, just more knowledgeable. But Roger also had three things working for him: He had volunteered for the facilitator's training, he didn't have the mind-set of "this won't work on my machine" (in fact, he had always felt there was a better way), and it wasn't his process that was being changed.

Triad Theorem 19: The full benefit of training in the systems and people circles requires interactions — that is, facilitating and coaching — from the direction circle after the training.

Using the unified total quality model to plan training does highlight some possible problems that are preventable during the planning stage. In this example with the 14 points for management, it is important to train management first. Training CQI teams in the 14 points can be disastrous if management has not bought into them or, worse yet, doesn't even know they exist. Contemplate a team trying to practice the methodology of continuous improvement in an environment in which management isn't practicing the 14 points. For example, how effective would the team be if management wasn't implementing point 8, drive out fear? In an environment of fear the CQI team members might have a hard time acquiring valuable information or process data on the extent of a problem and probably would feel constrained in the types of solutions they would present to management.

Management Action Supporting the TQM Triad

When we last visited the housekeeping CQI team, it was comparing its savings to net profit and an equivalent number of rooms rented. I'll bet a few of you were feeling uneasy about this insight, and a few more were thinking about what to do with this newfound information. The unasked question at that time, but maybe already being asked in your mind: Does the team deserve part of this net profit contribution as a bonus? Or more generally, how do we reward our teams, not give away the farm, and keep them motivated and productive? This would be an excellent time for me to employ the Socratic method of leaving you with these questions, because realistically you will have to invent your own workable solutions for your organization. There are more questions that need to be asked, and some "quicksand" areas to be pointed out.

Before we continue this line of questioning, maybe we should determine if we are even asking the right questions. In chapter 7 it was stated that if management could change the systems to capture the entire cost savings from the CQI project, it would become net profit. Before we concern ourselves with a reward for the team, we must first confront the design and implementation of these system changes. They must meet certain criteria: (1) maximize the capture of projected COQ savings and (2) reinforce the practice of TQM methodologies.

What management actions are taken now will affect the future direction of the organization's TQM effort. Sixty percent of the projected savings in the hotel project was related to labor savings. Therefore, to gain that portion of the savings, something must change with the labor input to the housekeeping operating system. Your organization may not be in the hotel business, but many CQI projects will come down to this same basic question. How do we reduce our labor costs that theoretically have been eliminated by this CQI project? Take the wrong tack here, and your TQM effort is most assuredly doomed. Who will want to help on the next CQI team if the last project resulted in a 10 percent staff reduction? How can we justify laying off dedicated people who figured out how to increase net profit by 37 percent?

We have arrived at a seeming dichotomy. One basic objective of management actions is to increase net profit. The CQI process appears to be a powerful methodology for doing that. We need excited, empowered employees to operate the CQI process—but we need to reduce the staff size to gain the results. Talk about a rock and a hard place!

We must build trust and net profit together. Quality profits dictate this. Remember that the operational definition for quality profits (see chapter 4) stated that one of the three methods for measurement is an increase in the internal customer satisfaction index. Also, to paraphrase triad theorem 11 in chapter 4, a methodology in one circle (in this case, CQI in the systems circle) cannot be undermined by an activity in another circle (in this case, layoffs in the direction circle).

Cost of Quality and Management Action

Let's review the $46,800 per year in labor savings in the hotel project to see if there is a way out of this dilemma. (Table 7.1 is repeated here as Table 8.1 for reference purposes.)

Table 8.1: *4-Star Hotel housekeeping CQI team COQ report.*

Assumptions

Staff:	20 housekeepers
Wages and benefits:	$10 per hour
Work week:	40 hours
Cleaning rate:	1 room per hour

All costs and calculations on a per-week basis.

Total labor costs:
    20 housekeepers × 40 hours × $10 per hour = $8000

Total rooms cleaned:
    20 housekeepers × 40 hours × 1 room per hour = 800 rooms

Total receipts:
    800 rooms × $100 per room = $80,000

Complaint call information:
    80 complaints per week, 60 called in, 40 missing-item calls

Item	Calculation	Failure COQ	Potential savings
1	10% savings in labor costs × $8000 =		$800
2	Time on phone: 60 calls × 2 minutes (.033 hours) × $10 =	20	
3	Delivering missing items: 40 × 10 minutes (.167 hours) × $10 =	67	
4	Recleaning rooms: 5 per week × 1 hour × $10 =	50	
5	Discounts given to dissatisfied customers: 40 rooms × $20 =	800	
	Total failure COQ	$937	
	73 percent savings ($937 × .73)		684
	Total potential savings per week		$1484

The first item represents the highest potential for savings and is due to the reduction of the housekeeping staff by two. In the case of the hotel, employee turnover can be utilized to effect the staff decrease. Staff turnover had been reduced from the industrywide figure of more than 100 percent to a low of 53 percent two years after full implementation of the TQM system. At this level of turnover the 10 percent reduction can still be handled without a layoff. In other industries where the turnover may be quite low, this solution of waiting for employees to quit may not be viable. Placement in other job openings within the organization, early retirement packages, or whatever the solution, it must meet the constraint of preserving internal customer satisfaction. One approach is to select the best CQI team members and turn them into full-time CQI team facilitators with a guarantee of returning to their original jobs within a stated period of time. Admittedly, this does not reduce labor costs in the short term, but it's similar to reinvesting earned interest to gain the advantages of compounding your investment.

The real point, which I probably obliterated with this discussion, is not *how* to reduce the workforce size, but *why* we are doing it. Most downsizing occurs because of mandated cuts—you must reduce costs and improve profits quickly! Those who survive take on the added work of those who did not. The hotel, however, must reduce staff not because of a mandate, but because process improvements have eliminated the work. That is a huge distinction. It might be argued that it's the difference between panic management of a company slowly going out of business and wise management of a growing company. Certainly the mandated scenario is not self-sustaining. One can only wonder how many of the panic situations could have been averted if management had been serious about the TQM efforts.

TQM efforts at cost reduction, however, are self-sustaining—team successes building team successes. The result is not a staff doing more with less and producing disappointing outcomes, whether in quality, quantity, or on-time delivery.

Items 2 through 4 (see Table 8.1) represent the balance of the labor cost savings. This type of cost savings is quite common in CQI projects. The time saved is in small, randomly dispersed segments and as such can't be readily captured by staff reduction. For example, even though the total time spent dealing with complaints on the telephone was two hours, it was distributed into unplanned two-minute segments, on the average. If telephoned complaints were completely eliminated, someone on the hotel staff wouldn't discover an unused two-hour block of time. I recommend continuing to document these segments as CQI project cost savings potential, as opposed to cost savings captured. The difference between these two totals, potential and captured, can be reconciled in three ways.

1. Some of this elusive time savings can be applied to the additional time required by CQI team meetings. Item 4 represents 3.65 hours saved [5 hours × 73 percent]. This equates to three housekeepers spending more than an hour each week in team meetings.
2. The savings resulting from items 2 and 3 could affect productivity. The time is now available for value-added work.
3. If it looks as if there is absolutely no way to capture the savings or gain a measurable benefit from it, the potential savings still represents a reduction in stress in the organization. That two minutes per complaint call, 60 times per week will be a welcome cost avoidance.

Stay the Course

The standard scenario in one organization continually beat down the TQM system. Management talked quality improvement, but rewarded the opposite.

When a process broke down and a delivery to a major customer was in jeopardy of being delayed to the point of causing the company to suffer financial consequences, the fire fighting commenced. Machinists and assemblers worked overtime; support personnel in engineering, marketing, and shipping worked far into the night; and finally a special truck would be dispatched with the overdue order.

The group responsible for the heroic display of quick fixing was recognized for its efforts, and that was the end of it until the next process failure. No analysis followed, no effort was made to move past the quick fix, and no CQI team was formed to ensure that this seemingly monthly occurrence never happened again.

Triad Theorem 20: Reward the heroic efforts of quick fixing a failed process, but recognize the signal for a continuous improvement opportunity.

Another aspect of staying the course is not jumping from program to program. Always jumping on the latest buzzword bandwagon doesn't accomplish anything except wearing out the organization with needless change and upheaval. Go back to the beginning, do each correctly, install permanently—then build from there. If an organization had implemented TQM in the mid-1980s and consistently held a 10 percent payoff, or even 5 percent, compare that to not doing anything and now having to get a 30 percent to 40 percent payoff immediately. Lack of doing the hard but effective work year by year forces an organization to use layoffs and downsizing, both negative approaches to accomplish what could have been reached with the positive approach of increasing continuous improvement, customer satisfaction, and growth potential.

Where Do We Go from Here?

Develop Your Organization's Three-Circle Model

Here is one example approach. In the spirit of the flexibility of the unified total quality model, I invite you to design a unique one for your organization.

Step 1. List all the TQM-related programs that your organization has attempted to install.

Step 2. Place each program into the proper circle of the TQM triad.

Step 3. Identify which of the programs are now operating as effective processes. Probably just the last one implemented, right?

Step 4. Are there portions of or complete programs that need to be reinstated to provide balance in your model? Use the model to explain to others in your organization why some of the previous programs/processes need to be restored to an effective state.

Step 5. Are there voids in your unified TQM system? Start the implementation of new programs by introducing them within the context of the model. Describe new training offered in terms of which circle is being addressed.

Step 6. Indicate the benefits of the new program and the expected interactions with the organization's present TQM system and processes.

Step 7. Continue to support the entire effort—not just the last program added.

Step 8. Celebrate your successes.

The total quality effort is like a building site where we are all builders in quality. Suppliers have been hauling in loads of building supplies for years. We get excited about each new delivery—this is *the* important key element to the structure. We start building anew, only to have it once again topple over or set idle. When will we stop looking for the one important key block and realize that all the elements are important? We can't build a TQM system that works with just one methodology any more than we can build a skyscraper with just glass or steel or concrete or electrical wire. Remember the system definition—it applies to the TQM system as well. A system is a group of interdependent elements...that together form a structure in which processes can operate. It's time to start building your unified total quality system.

 **Appendix**

The Triad Theorems

Triad Theorem 1: TQM is not three divergent methodologies forced together in a three-segment pie diagram, but three interlocking circles that interact with each other synergistically.

Triad Theorem 2: Every organization will take its own unique route to its own unique TQM system—throw away your cookbooks.

Triad Theorem 3: You pick the color, but make sure your TQM definition is an umbrella.

Triad Theorem 4: Actions in one circle that negatively impact the other two circles are counterproductive to TQM and produce nonquality outcomes.

Triad Theorem 5: A viable TQM system has the ability to continuously improve itself.

Triad Theorem 6: Managers, who work in the direction circle, need to understand the application of TQM programs in the other two circles.

Triad Theorem 7: What may be true or acceptable in one circle may be false or unacceptable in another circle.

Triad Theorem 8: Using a program in the wrong circle can be hazardous to an organization's health.

Triad Theorem 9: A program in one circle does not replace a program in another circle; they synergistically work together.

Triad Theorem 10: Quality program activities in the three triad circles must be balanced.

Triad Theorem 11: An activity, tool, or methodology in one circle should not negate, contradict, or undermine an activity, tool, or methodology in another circle.

Triad Theorem 12: The measures of success of the TQM triad level processes are found in the improved quality performance of processes at the operational level.

Triad Theorem 13: Success or failure is not measured in terms of percentage gain on only one project, but on long-term gains year after year.

Triad Theorem 14: A well-designed process in either the systems or people circle can fail without the support of the proper strategies from the direction circle.

Triad Theorem 15: A chart may be worth a thousand words, but action is worth a thousand charts.

Triad Theorem 16: Employees' attitudes while servicing external customers reflect the quality of customer service they receive as internal customers.

Triad Theorem 17: To gain the full advantage of synergism between processes, each process must be operating effectively.

Triad Theorem 18: Excellent customer service while righting a wrong, not followed and supported by continuous improvement, is no more than an expensive quick fix.

Triad Theorem 19: The full benefit of training in the systems and people circles requires interactions—that is, facilitating and coaching—from the direction circle after the training.

Triad Theorem 20: Reward the heroic efforts of quick fixing a failed process, but recognize the signal for a continuous improvement opportunity.

References

Ball, Melinda J. 1992. *Total Quality Transformation Improvement Tools*. Dayton, Ohio: PQ Systems.

Brassard, Michael. 1989. *The Memory Jogger Plus +™*: Featuring the Seven Management and Planning Tools. Methuen, Mass.: GOAL/QPC.

Brown, Mark Graham, Darcy E. Hitchcock, and Marsha L. Willard. 1994. *Why TQM Fails and What to Do About It*. New York: Irwin Professional Publishing.

Buch, Kimberly, and J. William Shelnutt. 1995. UNC Charlotte measures the effects of its quality initiative. *Quality Progress* 28 (July): 73–77.

Burns, Clarence. 1994. *Continuous Quality Improvement: Process Modeling, Problem Solving and SPC*. Marshalltown, Ia.: Burns Quality Systems.

Campanella, Jack, ed. 1990. *Principles of Quality Costs: Principles, Implementation, and Use*. 2d ed. Milwaukee: ASQC Quality Press.

Corrigan, James P. 1995. The art of TQM. *Quality Progress* 28 (July): 61–64.

Crosby, Philip B. 1984. *Quality Without Tears: The Art of Hassle-Free Management*. New York: New American Library.

Deming, W. Edwards. 1986. *Out of the Crisis*. Cambridge: MIT Center for Advanced Engineering Study.

Deming, W. Edwards. 1993. *The New Economics: For Industry, Government, Education*. Cambridge: MIT Center for Advanced Engineering Study.

Elbert, David. 1996. Tellers on duty on wheels. *Des Moines Register,* 11 September.

Frost, Roger. 1996. ISO guides, not governs, (a letter to the editor). *Quality* 35 (June): 124.

GOAL/QPC Research Committee. 1990. *Hoshin Planning: A Planning System for Implementing Total Quality Management (TQM)*. Methuen, Mass.: GOAL/QPC.

Goldratt, Eliyahu M. 1990. *Theory of Constraints.* Great Barrington, Mass.: North River Press.

Hammer, Michael, and James Champy. 1993. *Reengineering the Corporation: A Manifesto for Business Revolution.* New York: HarperCollins Publishers.

Hammer, Michael, and Steven A. Stanton. 1995. *The Reengineering Revolution: A Handbook.* New York: HarperCollins Publishers.

Hawking, Stephen W. 1988. *A Brief History of Time.* New York: Bantam Books.

Johnson, Elizabeth D. 1994. Re-engineering: Who, what, when, how, and how much? *The Quality Management Forum: The Newsletter for the Quality Management Division of the ASQC* 20 (Fall): 8–11.

Juran, J. M. 1989. *Juran on Leadership for Quality: An Executive Handbook.* New York: The Free Press.

Kelada, Joseph N. 1996. *Integrating Reengineering with Total Quality.* Milwaukee: ASQC Quality Press.

Landes, Les. 1995. Leading the duck at mission control. *Quality Progress* 28 (July): 43–48.

Latzko, William J., and David M. Saunders. 1995. *Four Days with Dr. Deming: A Strategy for Modern Methods of Management.* Reading, Mass.: Addison-Wesley.

Melum, Mara Minerva, and Casey Collett. 1995. *Breakthrough Leadership: Achieving Organizational Alignment Through Hoshin Planning.* Chicago: American Hospital Publishing.

NIST. 1997. *Malcolm Baldrige National Quality Award 1997 Criteria for Performance Excellence.* Gaithersburg, Md.: National Institute of Standards and Technology.

Peters, Tom. 1994. *The Tom Peters Seminar: Crazy Times Call for Crazy Organizations.* New York: Vintage Books.

———. 1995. Dumb and dumber. *Office Systems* 95 (February): 53.

Rau, Herbert. 1995. 15 years and still going. . . . *Quality Progress* 28 (July): 57–59.

Ritz-Carlton. 1993. *Malcolm Baldrige National Quality Award Application Summary.* Atlanta, Ga.: The Ritz-Carlton Hotel Company.

Roosevelt, Benjamin. 1995. Quality and business practices: Essential ingredients for success. *Quality Progress* 28 (July): 35–40.

Shapiro, Eileen C. 1995. *Fad Surfing in the Boardroom: Reclaiming the Courage to Manage in the Age of Instant Answers.* Reading, Mass.: Addison-Wesley.

Webster's Encyclopedic Unabridged Dictionary of the English Language. 1989. New York: Portland House.

Zeithaml, Valarie A., A. Parasuraman, and Leonard L. Berry. 1990. *Delivering Quality Service: Balancing Customer Perceptions and Expectations.* New York: The Free Press.

Index